The Accidental Chef:

A collection of recipes and the stories behind them

Joseph F. Caputo

© 2012 Joseph F. Caputo
All Rights Reserved.

No part of this publication may be reproduced, stored in a retrieval system, or transmitted, in any form or by any means, electronic, mechanical, photocopying, recording, or otherwise, without the written permission of the author.

First published by Dog Ear Publishing
4010 W. 86th Street, Ste H
Indianapolis, IN 46268
www.dogearpublishing.net

dog ear
PUBLISHING

ISBN: 978-1-4575-1211-7

This book is printed on acid-free paper.

Printed in the United States of America

DEDICATION

TO

THE TRUE AUTHORS

of

The Accidental Chef

My mother Mary Caputo

My grandfather Joseph Pizzola

My grandmother Angela Pizzola

My Heavenly Muses who inspire me

to cook, to love and to write

Now is the moment
to share the fruit of the gifts they have given me, and
to honor them by presenting
the pages which follow,
borne of some tears but also with great joy

Grazie Mille
To my wife Mary Ann
The author of so many happy years
Who continues to inspire me to love and to share

To my father Frank Caputo
And
My sister Rosemary
Lifetime beacons of love and support

MENU

AMUSE BOUCHE 1
STARTERS 3
STEPPING OUT OF MY MOTHER'S KITCHEN 6
TAKING CENTER STAGE 14
INTERMEZZO 17
ONE ENTRÉE AT A TIME 18
    THE RICE STORY 18
    THE PRIME RIB LOCK OUT 21
    TAKE IT OFF: EPISODE ONE 27
    HALF BEEF WILL TRAVEL 29
    FALLING "INTO THE SOUP" 31
    TO ZUPPA 35
    THE SALAD DRESSING DEAL 36
    COOLING OFF FROM THE HEAT OF THE KITCHEN 38
    A DREAM REALIZED 39
    JOE VERSES THE VOLCANO 42
    NOW YOU SEE IT—NOW YOU DON'T 44
    TAKE IT OFF: EPISODE TWO 46
    STAR STRUCK 49
    THE BEEF THAT GOT AWAY 53
    THE BABY—-OUT WITH THE BATH WATER 55
    IT'S ALIVE! 56

CELEBRATING THE PAST ON SEVERAL LEVELS 59
        ARRIVEDERCI PESCE OR GOODBYE FISH
DESSERT: THE ICING ON THE CAKE 61
RETURN TO "LA DOLCE VITA" 61
RECIPE SECTION INDEX 65
RECIPE SECTION 69

ACKNOWLEDGEMENTS

To my editor, Ellen Franco who painstakingly read and reread every word I have written.
    Without her dedication to clarity and detail, this book would never have come to fruition.

To my photographer Dino DeNaples who generated amazing photos.
    His creative energy was a motivating force throughout the process.

To Bruce Stein, my sous chef who always believed in what I was cooking.
    His constant support and continued encouragement kept me eager to continue.

To Tony Nicosia Jr., my best friend who is my brother and lifelong friend.
    During this endeavor and for years of believing in me, even when I didn't believe in myself, he has my unwavering gratitude.

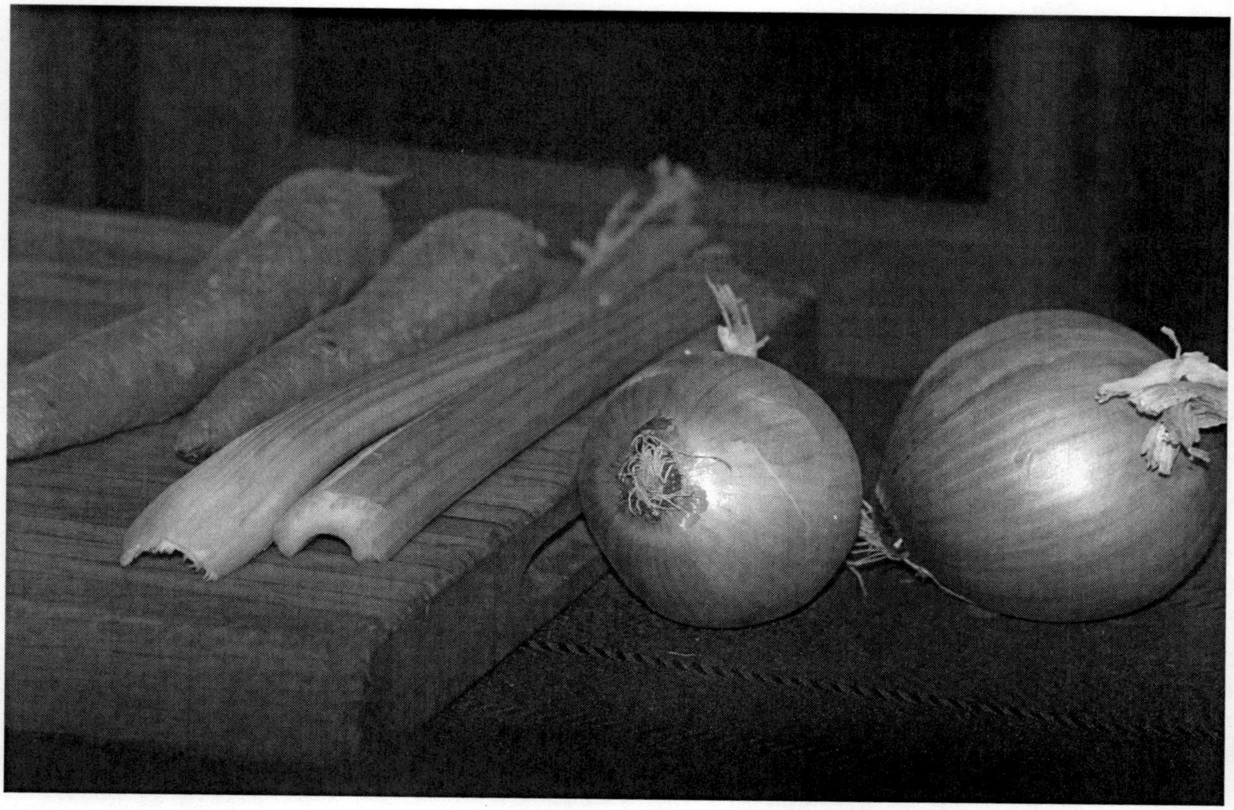

AMUSE BOUCHE

The ingredients were there all along. I assumed that everyone had those same ingredients in the cupboards and pantries of their own psyches—just as I had them in mine. I thought that everyone could take a little bit of this and a little bit of that, and in a very short time come up with something not only edible, but also delicious. What came to me as second nature was something I thought everybody else also had tucked in their own bag of "fun things to do."

How was I to know that as a little boy, hanging on my grandmother's and mother's apron strings in the sanctuaries of their kitchens would one day change my life?

How was I to know that watching and helping my grandfather in his garden and in his canning cellar would ultimately play a very important role in my life—but only after a half century of my being somewhat oblivious to the gifts I had been given?

Someone once said to me that the only certainty in life is change. Strange or seemingly contradictory, the truth of that adage is evident in my life and maybe in yours too. When life changing events happen to people at any age, but especially as we get older, starting over seems frightening and even impossible. When I was fifty years old, I lost my position as principal of a local school. Furthermore, I was not offered any other position in the system, although for twenty years previous to working in administration, I had been a teacher in that same system. For me, losing my place in an educational system to which I had dedicated so many years of my life was, to say the least, disturbing.

There is a bright side, however, a really bright side. Through those events that forced me into making a major career change, I've learned much, much about my gifts, much about myself. No doubt, seeking comfort, I turned to the things that I remembered from childhood—fond memories of my maternal grandparents and my mother—their cooking, the love we shared through their nourishing and nurturing dishes. I began to formulate a plan. The changes I was forced to make as I redirected my energies into choosing a new and fulfilling career did not come without hardships. Yet, those difficulties made it clear to me that adversity can create miracles. Starting over can be an exciting journey in self realization and awareness. Now that I am enjoying such a journey, I want to share it with you.

Presently, I am the owner of two successful businesses in the food industry: "*Catering by Joseph*," and a restaurant subdivision "*Zuppa del Giorno.*"

I also have been a guest chef for a major cruise line on many occasions.

After beginning those enterprises and enjoying a great deal of success, someone said to me, "You were just lucky!"

I took great offense at that statement. I never attributed good things in my life to luck. I knew I had a wonderful childhood, a great family, a loving wife, a good home, and, of course, good health. Luck? Accident? I don't think so! Blessings, yes! Yet at fifty, when I found myself jobless, I had to face a practical problem, and solve it effectively. I had to find a new niche in life in order for me to be fulfilled, happy, and might I add, capable of making a living.

At times, this period was painful. It involved a lot of hard work, maybe the hardest work I had ever done in my life. It's still hard work, but I chose to throw myself into the area I loved best—-the area I took for granted—-the area that never merited a place among possible career choices when I was a young man. At fifty, I chose to cook for a living. It seemed so odd. I would do what I "loved to do most," and it would be my "job." I would earn a living doing the thing I most loved to do.

True, cooking is physically demanding and extraordinarily time consuming. Yet, I know this: I don't want to do anything else. I do want to cook for the rest of my life.

I remember how funny it was the first day I put on a chef coat, pants and toque! I looked in the mirror and I laughed. From business suit to this? Did I fit the part? I looked silly, but once I walked into that commercial kitchen, I was right at home. I let go. Doors began to open. Things began to unfold. I picked up the chef knife and began to prepare one of countless meals that so many people have since enjoyed.

I'd like you to enjoy them too.

Read on, and you too can create. You too can be the recipient of my mother's, my grandmother's, my grandfather's, and my own love affair with food.

I hope it will be as much fun for you as it has been for me.

STARTERS

Some middle-aged men buy sports cars or motorcycles when they turn fifty. Others have hair transplants or run away with a younger woman. I decided that I was going to open a catering business and maybe even a restaurant.

After twenty years of serving primarily as an educator in a Catholic school system, along with holding other supplemental jobs, I was informed that the school in which I had been principal would close the following year. I was encouraged to reapply for my job. I did, but I was not rehired. I was devastated. Several years before the announcement of the closing, somewhere in the back of my mind, I had the idea that if ever I had the opportunity, or if ever the school closed as many other Catholic schools in the area had, I might cook for a living.

The idea of cooking was not novel to me. I had always cooked. As a youngster, I watched my mother and my grandparents cook with great interest. As I grew older I used to help them to prepare food for many traditional family feasts that I had grown so accustomed to.

One of my early creations for mom's parties

Growing up, I was drawn to any cooking show that was on television. During my grade school and high school years, Julia Child was a great inspiration to me as I watched her public television show "The French Chef." I would spend many Saturdays also watching other cooking shows. I fondly remember many of those afternoons sitting with my mother or grandmother and enjoying those shows. Later, I would pester them, insisting that I could make the dish that we had seen prepared earlier that day on television.

Cooking was an essential part of our family life. With great patience and care, and, I am sure, with some pride, my mother and grandmother enabled me to grasp at a very young age the principles of cooking which they themselves had mastered through the repetition and practice of cooking countless meals for our family. When my mother entertained guests, I would often help, and sometimes prepare the whole meal myself.

Even for holidays and other special occasions, my grandparents were always willing to allow me to lend a hand with the food preparation and cooking. I have treasured those moments my entire life.

Sunday dinners—endless bowls of pasta, baked macaroni, roasted chicken, veal cutlets and braciole—were a regular weekly ritual. I ate those meals with great relish and delight. Food was an integral part of who we were and the love we shared with one another.

Homemade Pasta in my mother's kitchen

My mother Mary and especially her teacher, my grandmother Angela, were masters at making pasta. Once either or both had prepared the meal, they joined the family and enjoyed the meal with us.

I watched and learned how to make ravioli, lasagna, manicotti, and fettuccine. My grandfather Joseph Pizzola made the most delicious meatballs. My grandmother's meatballs were different but also fantastic. On countless Sundays of my childhood, I remember distinguishing just who did the cooking that particular day. Stealing a meatball after Sunday Mass or dunking a small piece of Italian bread into a bubbling pot of Sunday tomato sauce, always betrayed the secret of just who was in charge of the kitchen that day.

Besides expressing his talent in the kitchen, my grandfather also had a beautiful garden. He would grow the most marvelous vegetables: tomatoes, peppers, corn, green beans, and zucchini. The abundant parsley, basil and mint he grew complemented the wonderful dishes he would concoct.

I don't know what his secret was, but Grandpa Pizzola's garden was truly amazing. As children, my sister Rosemary and I would get lost in the corn as it grew higher and higher. The only time that was better than playing in the garden was the time we spent eating the bounty that came from it!

My grandfather in his garden

I was always what I would like to call "chubby." Since we lived in the apartment above my grandparents, I would walk into their kitchen at supper time and partake of their evening meal. "EAT!" my grandparents would announce as I entered the kitchen from the back door of the house. Sometimes I would hear the equally familiar command in Italian, "Mangia!"

"I'll just taste a little, Grandma. I know my mother is cooking."

Later, I would climb the inside staircase to my mother's kitchen where I enjoyed a second supper.

Grandma and me at her kitchen table

I fondly remember those double suppers: my grandfather's veal cutlets that were most times made of venison, his minestra, and zucchini stew, or my grandmother's fried potatoes, polenta, spinach and potatoes. Simple dishes, but even now I can almost taste those marvelous flavors.

As I ascended the inside stairs to my mother's kitchen, one by one, the aroma of her fried chicken, her meatloaf, and her Swiss steak became deeply embedded in my olfactory memory.

"Did you eat downstairs?" Mom would ask. "Just a taste," I'd reply, as I'd watch her remove a freshly baked loaf of one of many types of homemade breads from its pan. Nothing was ever more inviting to a little boy who was always hungry and looking for something delicious to eat. Enticed by the magical aroma of the bread, I always had the courage to snatch a piece, dip it into whatever deliciousness Mom had bubbling on the stovetop and wait for her reaction of delight when I told her it was the best loaf ever.

My grandparents' home, our home for most of my life

THE ACCIDENTAL CHEF

STEPPING OUT OF MY MOTHER'S KITCHEN

My mother posing at the stove

Me in mom's kitchen

My mother was a wonderful cook. She cooked whenever she could. Because she spent most of her life working in a garment factory, Sunday was "cook for the week" day. On Sundays, she cooked the usual pasta dinner, but on the four burners of her electric stove there were always multiple pots of temptations simmering, boiling, frying or braising. She would cook four or five dishes for the week and then store them in the refrigerator for suppers that she would serve when she came home from work.

Besides cooking at home, Mom and I were often in New York City where we sampled the foods of one fine restaurant or another. We visited *Sardi's, Tavern on the Green, The Rainbow Room, The Sign of the Dove, Patricia Murphy's, Windows on the World, The Top of the Sixes, The Red Coach Grill at the Sheraton, Joe's Pier 52 at the Americana, Downey's Steakhouse,* and *The Russian Tea Room.* These are just a few of the well known restaurants that I fondly remember from my trips to New York City.

At home, I eventually became acquainted with what I still

Joseph F. Caputo

consider a local restaurant with dishes comparable to those I had enjoyed in the city. On many occasions my dad Frank Caputo would take the family out to celebrate a special event or to give my mother a break from the kitchen. Invariably, he would chose a nearby restaurant called *Billy's Seafood and Steakhouse* owned by a friend of his. I loved going to *Billy's*. The food was amazing and Billy was quite a character.

I can honestly say I was in awe of him. Little did I know how my relationship with him would develop and how he would influence my future.

. . .AND STEPPING INTO MY FIRST COMMERCIAL KITCHEN

Billy's Seafood and Steakhouse

When I was 16, my father decided that it was time for me to have a part time job. Dad had already taught me responsibility and instilled in me a very strong work ethic. What better choice for my father than to call on his friend Billy who just happened to need a dishwasher. Dad took me to see him at his restaurant, but this time not for dinner. Dad had plans to land me a job with Billy.

That afternoon, Billy appeared to me in a different light. He was a formidable figure, good looking, heavy set, and somewhat sophisticated with his distinguished moustache. For the first time he appeared to be austere. What I came to discover years later was that this man really helped shape my experience with "front of the house" and "back of the house" operations in a restaurant. *Billy's Seafood and Steakhouse* was a vibrant business. Moreover, Billy really liked me and I loved working in his restaurant.

"You want him to wash dishes?" he incredulously asked my father.

My father was speechless, a rarity for him. Finally he blurted out, "Your newspaper ad said you need a dishwasher."

"He belongs in the front!" Billy announced. "He'll start as a busboy."

I don't know what he saw or what he liked about me, but Billy saw some panache in me to be in the front of the house. "He belongs up front with me," he repeated. Boy, was I glad because I hated to wash dishes!

He took me in the back of the kitchen and let me try on several crisply starched white coats. "That one fits you well," he announced. "You have black pants?"

"Yes," I replied.

"Be here at 4 p.m. on Friday. We'll get you started."

My dad drove me to *Billy's* at 3:45 p.m. on Friday. I insisted on being on time. "Good luck," he said as I exited the car and quickly made my way into the front of the restaurant.

Billy's had a sort of stage that patrons walked onto as they entered the dining room of the restaurant.

It was a raised platform with two steps that led down into the dining room. I stopped for a moment on that level and observed the entire dining room from that vantage point.

The dining room had a large banquette that was situated in the lower right corner of the room. The banquette was shaped in a triangle and seated six people. Sometimes when the restaurant was really jumping, two additional chairs were added in front of the table to seat eight. To the left of this area at the edge of the bottom step sat a huge Hammond organ.

Next to the banquette were two large round tables that seated six. To the left of the farther round table were two deuces. A deuce seats two people. These were my favorite tables because they sat against a wooden art deco rail that bordered the huge rounded "U" shaped bar. The bar was made of a Plexiglas type material that resembled onyx. About a dozen black leather swivel chairs that were used as bar stools surrounded the bar.

The area past the two deuces and to the right, directly in front of the bar, was known as the "cocktail lounge." The lounge had a series of about four deuces along the wall. The men's room was at the end of that wall. It was very small. There were shutters that gave privacy to a patron and obstructed the view from the bar as the door was opened. "Ice those urinals!" Billy would command the bartenders. Despite the fact that the urinals had camphor cakes in them, Billy kept the urinals iced so as to keep the men's room fresh and clean, especially since the facility was so close to the bar and the cocktail lounge. I always found it comical to watch one of the bartenders fill a bucket with ice and then enter the men's room. I wondered what the customers thought.

Anyone walking from the cocktail lounge into the main dining room itself saw a small banquette for two directly near the kitchen door. Then perpendicular to the kitchen entrance were a series of four booths that were set two by two, separated by a large water fountain illuminated with multicolored lights that would change from hues of red and blue and then to those of green and gold. This scenario created ambiance and charm comparable to one in an Italian piazza.

The last wall of the restaurant sat a table of six next to another banquette for two. I loved this part of the restaurant as lighted flower boxes of ferns ran along that wall. As patrons made their way to the entrance, again there was another mirrored wall with another round for six. Smack in the middle of the room were two rectangular shaped tables, one running horizontally and the other vertically. These additional tables could seat six or eight customers.

On Friday and Saturday nights, the place was packed. A man named Elio played the Hammond organ, and a very dark haired woman, Sara Marie, obviously of Italian descent, played a cocktail combo drum and sang. The duo would begin every program with *"Arrivederci Roma."* When the song began the staff knew it was time to hustle. Sara Marie's melodic voice would ring out … "Arrivederci Roma, good bye, good bye to Rome…" One of the waitresses named Big Jean would announce, "Here we go!" Big Jean was sort of the sage of the place. She rarely got angry even in the craziest situations. No matter how chaotic a particular night may have unfolded, the staff was usually cheerful and amicable with each other until night's end. With her big smile and deep voice, Big Jean would announce, "It's like I always say; it all works out at the end of the night!"

That first night, when Billy saw me on the entrance platform taking the place in, he announced, "You're here, kid!" He called me "kid" endearingly sometimes, but for the most part he called me Joe. I hated Joe.

"His name is Joseph," was my mother's quick correction of anyone who called me Joe. This was my first day of work and I was not about to tell Billy that my mother preferred that her son be called by his proper name. At *Billy's*, I knew I'd be answering to Joe.

Billy began to escort me through the double kitchen doors of the dining room which led to a space he called the "cubby." It was a long rectangular pantry and it housed the coffee makers, ice cream cooler and another cooler where cream for coffee, butter, whipped cream and other perishables were kept. The space also had long shelves on the walls where linens were stacked along with some of the many dishes and glasses.

Billy took one of his signature gold napkins, a water glass, a knife, two forks, and a teaspoon along with a cup and saucer. "Follow me," he ordered.

He led me out to the dining room and brought me to the long vertical table directly outside the kitchen door. The table was partially set. Two middle aged women were nervously scurrying as they set the table in the presence of their boss. "Girls, this is Joe, our new busboy," he proudly announced.

The girls' names were Rose and Peggy. They seemed nice and it was my understanding that Billy would pay me 90 cents an hour and all the girls were to give me a small portion of their tips. I smiled and said "Hello." I knew my salary depended on their liking me.

"I'm going to show you how to set a table 'my way,'" Billy said. From the looks on the faces of the two women, it was obvious we were all about to get a lesson in table setting.

Billy stood in front of one of the captain's chairs and placed the salad and dinner forks on the left side of the table with the larger fork just a bit higher than the smaller. He proceeded to place the water glass on the upper right above the butter knife, blade facing in, and the teaspoon to the right of the knife. The cup and saucer sat directly right of the teaspoon.

He meticulously folded the starched gold napkin into a triangle that had a creased slit in front and set the triangle with the creased slit facing out. "You fold it like this," he instructed while he unfolded one of the other napkins at the place setting next to the one on which he was working, and handed it to me. Unfolding the napkin he had just folded, he began to refold the linen showing me precisely how to arrive at the triangle with the perfectly creased slit. "Good," he announced as I showed him my napkin. I could hear a phone ringing. "Help the girls finish setting this table," he instructed, and left me with the girls as he went into the bar area to answer the phone.

I will never forget one Saturday night when we were really busy; it was rare not to be jammed on a Saturday night. The place was buzzing with customers. We kept turning tables over and over as soon as they were available. Sara Marie and Elio were at their peak performance: *"Granada...";* *"Maliguena...";* *"Volare...";* *"Femmina."* Sara Marie was singing them all. The phone was ringing off the hook.

Billy took one particular call and when he hung up he began to move tables in the cocktail lounge. He frantically began to separate several tables that were bumped together to accommodate more diners. I ran over to help him. "Girls, girls," he called. "Doctor . . . is coming!" By the way Billy was acting, I thought the Pope was coming!

THE ACCIDENTAL CHEF

I came to find out later that the doctor was a renowned cardiologist in the area and Billy was eager to give Doctor the best. "Joe, get the Jazz," he ordered. Jazz was a dish of cottage cheese mixed with chives and another dish of white cannellini beans with diced white onion mixed with a homemade Italian dressing. We served Jazz along with an iced boat of carrots, split scallions, and celery. Of course, crusty Italian bread, assorted crackers, breadsticks and butter accompanied the Jazz.

We had to be very careful when filling the small monkey dishes with Jazz from iced containers that sat just inside the inner kitchen doors. If beans or cottage cheese fell into the water of the melting ice, Billy would scowl as he pointed to the floating cannellini, "See those beans; that's my money floating away!"

When someone would come to the restaurant very late, Billy, sometimes exhausted, would announce, "Joe, get them a table, and cut the Jazz." That meant that they didn't get any. They came too late.

For the most part, Billy was very, very fair, but sometimes he manipulated the system to give the customer and his restaurant the maximum advantage. Like I said, he was the master. The man was a brilliant restaurateur.

But the first night was the best! I was introduced to Jean, Big Jean, Irene, Sally, and Eileen. I had already met Rose and Peggy.

The girls showed me the ropes. It was hard work lifting the trays of dirty dishes, but I loved it.

"Let me show you how to stack a tray 'my way,'" Billy said as he approached me while I was clearing the dirty dishes off a large table of six. A large oval tray always covered with a signature gold napkin sat on a tray jack adjacent to the kitchen door.

"You take a plate," he said, "and you scrape the uneaten food onto it." As he did what he was saying, he accidentally dropped a small piece of baked potato from the plate onto the floor. "Eileen," he called as he snapped his fingers. "When you have the time." He pointed to the fallen food on the floor. Eileen, with napkin in hand, retrieved the potato skin almost immediately and placed it on the tray.

Billy continued, "Then stack all the similar plates together, and be sure to balance the tray. Keep the plates on the ends of the oval tray, keep the glasses and the silverware in the middle, linens on top. When you lift the tray, bend your knees and hoist the tray up over your shoulder."

I did exactly as Billy had instructed. He looked proud as his new bus boy gracefully carried the full tray up and over his shoulder. All the girls carried those trays in a similar fashion and he chided the ones who could not lift them up. Big Jean carried the trays best. As the larger tables sometimes had two servers, the server who could hoist the tray usually carried the tray out of the kitchen. As I got more familiar with the girls and their tips, I would offer to carry out the trays whenever they had difficulty.

After a few weekends, I was a pro. I had so much fun. The girls, most middle aged women, old enough to be my mother, would joke and laugh with me as we squeezed ourselves into the small "cubby." We reached for glasses, scooped out ice cream, grabbed linens, and filled carafes of coffee. Indeed, these were very tight quarters. We were constantly bumping against each other, and we thought that all the proximity among six or seven women and one high school boy was all very funny.

Two years later, when I turned 18, Billy announced, "It's time to promote you to waiter." I was ready!

I followed the girls with water pitchers to fill empty glasses. I carried their heavy trays brimming with steaming house specialties like Shrimp Scampi, Chicken Strips in Wine and Butter, Live Stuffed Lobster, Filet Mignon and Veal Française. I cleared table after table; I poured coffee and I helped them make ice cream parfaits in the small cubby. Without question, Crème de Menthe was my favorite parfait.

"Girls, watch that ice cream," Billy commanded. "My accountant told me, 'Be careful! A little scoop here and a little scoop there—-before you know it, it all adds up!'"

I was the only waiter in the restaurant and the customers tipped me very well. Billy taught me how to do Russian service, a style of serving that is almost nonexistent in restaurants today. With Russian service the food is prepared in the kitchen but then brought to the table on a platter or other serving tray or vessel and then served to the guest tableside.

One of my favorite table side services was for Trout Amandine. The whole trout was on a platter and brought to a tray stand near the table of the guest I was serving. It was only in later years after I had experience as a chef that I learned that cooking fish on the bone was a European tradition. When I was eighteen, I had no idea that the best flavor was developed using this cooking method. I thought it was just a show to amuse the patrons.

Taking a large spoon, Billy showed me how to remove the head and tail of the fish. Then he showed me how to split the trout along its back with the spoon and then with the fork. A quick flip ensured that the fish would open into two perfect fillets. One more use of the fork, and the entire spine of bones was removed from the tail to the head of the fish. Then, the fish, still on the platter, was served to the waiting guest.

We also did Russian service for such dishes as Chicken Parmesan, Chicken Strips in Butter and Garlic and Chicken Strips in Wine and Mushrooms. The steaming casseroles of chicken would be brought to the table. Billy showed me how to use the service spoon and fork in combination, just like a set of tongs. I put on quite a performance, and I loved the show!

I hustled like crazy and made as much or more in tips as the women who had worked there for years. I had youth on my side and, of course, *a magnetic personality*. Also, I loved serving people and making them happy. I still do.

Billy was fair with all his employees, but he favored me, and I knew it. Then too, he also leaned on me to do things he didn't ask the others to do. Billy rarely sat; he was the maître d'! In later years, as he was aging, I noticed he would tire more easily. Sometimes he would take a seat near his table. Dressed in his grey suit, he still had an aura of class.

He would call me over from his seat, "Joe..." He motioned with his hand for me to come closer. "Tell them to lower that!" He meant the music. Sometimes Elio and Sara Marie would get a bit too loud for him. Another night when he was feeling nostalgic, he would say, "Tell them to play *'La Mama.'*" Sara would sing, "When the evening shadows fall and the lovely day is through./ Then with longing I recall the years I spent with you./ Mama solo per te la mia canzone vola/ Mama sarai con me tu non sarai piu sola" (Mama for you my song only flies/ Mama you will be with me/ you will not be alone any more)

After a very busy night, Billy, sitting at the bar as he often did when the restaurant finally settled down, would say "Have a drink." Billy often made this offer during the time I worked for him. He always told the bartender to get me a soda.

One night in April was different. As I had recently turned 21 years of age, Billy asked the bartender to mix me whatever I wanted. I think I had a White Russian. It was half and half mixed with Kahlua. Many Saturday nights after that, he would say, "Have a drink." I would choose whatever I wanted. He was so good to me and to all his staff.

It was a ritual that after every shift, the cooks in the kitchen would cook dinner for the wait staff. Sometimes we ordered just about anything off the menu, within reason of course. The Shrimp Scampi was my favorite. Sometimes when the cooks were in a really good mood or Billy was feeling exceptionally generous, he would have them prepare prime rib for all of us.

We sat at the back booths near the kitchen door just like a big family. I remember those dinners. Those chefs could really cook. One that I loved in particular was Tony. He would always tease me about one thing or another. One time I had gone to the shore and came back with severe sunburn. "Hey, what the sun fall on ya?" he shouted from over the steam table. It was Tony who really showed me how to cook like a professional. I watched everything he did; later I went home and cooked just as I had seen him do.

One time, Tony had a huge vat of Clams Casino sitting right inside the kitchen doors. I think the cooks were finishing up and then the Clams Casino was to be transferred to the cooler. In any event, I had on a new pair of shoes that did not have rubber soles. I entered through the swinging kitchen doors and, needless to say, slipped forward. I lost my balance and fell head first into the open vat of the clam stuffing.

Chuck, one of Tony's sous chefs came over and asked quite calmly, "How's the Clams Casino?"

My hair, my face, and part of my white coat were covered in the savory mixture. With my finger, I took some stuffing from my face, put my finger in my mouth, and shouted, "Hey, Ton, the Clams Casino needs more salt!" He cursed at me as he gave me a wet towel to clean myself up. He also handed me a new white coat; slip or not, the night's work wasn't over.

After many good years at *Billy's*, it was a sad day when I came to tell Billy that in June, I would graduate from college and probably move to New York City.

"We're gonna miss you, kid," he said.

"I'll miss you and I'll miss working in this place."

Life went on.

Twenty years later, I received a phone call from Billy's daughter Rosaria. She told me that Billy had passed away and she asked me if I would sing at her father's funeral. I was so moved. I told her how much her father meant to me and how he had impressed me with his skill, passion, and work ethic for the restaurant business. In spite of how austere a man Billy was, I told her that everything I had learned about the restaurant business, I had learned at *Billy's*. I loved the place and I loved her father.

I did sing at Billy's funeral. Afterwards, I spoke to his daughter and to his wife Josie. I told them the story of the first day I had met Billy and how he said to me, "You belong up front with me!"

And knowing that Billy had passed, I knew that God said the same thing to him.

I could not write about people who have taught me to love the art of cooking and fail to mention Billy. If Billy could hear my words, I'm sure he would dismiss them with his characteristically humble approach and tell me to "Cut the Jazz," and we all know exactly what that means.

I want to assure you that in deference

to Billy, I will not cut the Jazz. That recipe, along with

other recipes I stored in my memory and have only recently re-created from those

I enjoyed at *Billy's* restaurant, as well as many others can be found

in the Recipe Section of this book.

TAKING CENTER STAGE

Catering by Joseph

Despite the fact that I loved working at *Billy's*, the thought of culinary as a profession had not entered my mind during those early years. I loved to eat and I loved to cook, but the reality was that I had aspirations of becoming an actor or a singer. I earned a degree in Theatre from Marywood College and moved to New York City in the hopes of pursuing an acting career. During that time I felt isolated, unsuccessful and unhappy.

New York City was a lonely place for me. Though I loved the theatre and enjoyed performing, I hated the struggle of an actor's life. After less than a year and a half, I decided to return home.

When I returned home, I wrote a one man show with a few songs and some stories. I needed someone to play the piano for me. A very nice woman I had known over the years agreed to do that for me. Her name was Ann Marie.

Ann Marie and I traveled all over the area to women's clubs and luncheons, to Rotary and Elks dinners to perform the show. These performances sustained me for a period until I was hired as an elementary school teacher in a Catholic school. I did continue, however, to work with Ann Marie and moonlight as a performer to augment my teaching salary.

One day I invited Ann Marie to lunch. I did not have much money to pay her as my accompanist and I thought I would take her to lunch as a gesture of my appreciation. We enjoyed a nice lunch at a nearby restaurant and began to chat about the show, her children, and my changing career opportunities in various fields. My one man show was enjoying success on the local circuit, but I was doubtful that it had much more potential of attracting a wider audience.

Ann Marie and I talked and laughed about some of the events that we had enjoyed while performing. Suddenly, Ann Marie looked at her watch and became quite anxious.

"I have to go," she exclaimed. "My husband is having guests over for dinner and I haven't even thought about what I am going to serve."

"I'll do it," I said.

"You?"

"Yes, I can cook." I had worked at *Billy's* since I was 16, and continued to work there throughout my college years. Also I worked in various other restaurants at home and in New York even after I had landed my day jobs. Ann Marie was unaware of this aspect of my life. "Trust me, I can do this. Just give me some money and

Joseph F. Caputo

go home and get yourself and the house ready. She agreed and handed me two hundred dollars. With my own money, I quickly paid the bill and the two of us left the restaurant.

Ann Marie headed home and I headed out to the nearest supermarket. I began to plan the menu in my mind. I had always liked veal dishes and one of my favorites was Veal Oscar, a dish I had eaten in Aruba while there with my girlfriend Mary Ann (whom I later married).

Another favorite of mine, French Onion Soup could be a starter for almost any dinner. I also saw some fresh carrots in the market. I thought I could steam them and even manage to do some roasted potatoes. I thought all of these accompaniments would go well with the very rich veal dish that consisted of sautéed veal, lump crabmeat, asparagus and a lovely sauce similar to Hollandaise. I had my menu. I would pick up a cheesecake at a local bakery and serve it with some fresh strawberries. I quickly gathered all my ingredients, stopped at the bakery and headed back to Ann Marie's house in order to begin my ministrations.

Ann Marie's table set for dinner

Once at her home, I was completely comfortable in her kitchen. She had already set the table, and as I unpacked the groceries, I began to tell her what I was planning to make and serve in about two hours.

Ann Marie stared in amazement as I began to whirl around the kitchen and to cook the meal for her, her husband and their guests. "Do you need anything?" she asked.

"No," I confidently replied. "Just do what you need to do to get yourself ready; I can handle this." She could tell by my tone and the manner in which I was working that I had the whole thing under control.

She left me to my devices and in about two hours the entire meal was just about ready to be served.

Her husband arrived with two other couples and I began to serve the meal as if the whole process was second nature to me (and maybe it was!)

"Ooos" and "Ahhs" circled the table as I presented the Gruyère encrusted bowls of steaming French Onion Soup. I could hear both of the women asking my friend, "Where did you find him? Would he do a party for me?"

By the time I was serving the coffee and store bought cheesecake, one of the women asked me for a business card. "I don't have one," I said. "I don't have a business; I did this as a favor to Ann Marie."

"Oh, you must do this for me," she exclaimed as she pulled out a pen and paper and began to write down her number. I reluctantly took the paper and put it in my pocket. I had no intention of ever calling her. But a few weeks later, I thought to myself, "I may be on to something here." I wasn't making that much money teaching school, and so I eventually called her and set up the details for a party to be catered later at her home. I reached back into my early years and decided since it was summer and green beans and fresh mint were in abundance that I would design a menu around my grandfather's green bean and potato salad with mint as a refreshing first course.

JOSEPH THE CATERER
Joseph Frank Caputo
Intimate, Elegant Parties
Gourmet Dinner, Buffet or Cocktail
For Info. Call (717) 961-0234

My first business card!

At that second presentation, the guests raved about the unique salad and the way I presented it. I was excited and flattered, and I enjoyed the entire process. I felt I had nothing to lose and maybe a lot to gain. A few days later, I had cards printed which said "Joseph the Caterer." I received a few more invitations to do more parties and even more invitations from those parties. Before I knew it, I had a catering business.

I guess you could say that that first evening at Ann Marie's was my debut on the culinary arts stage. I was on my way to becoming a professional caterer quite by accident. Or was it?

INTERMEZZO

During those early years, when I was teaching, sometimes on the elementary level, sometimes on the secondary level, a series of events led me to make a rather important decision. Since my days spent at Marywood College, I remained connected to many people on the local theatre scene, and was well known around the community. While still doing my teaching, and catering parties, I was approached by a representative of Penn State's satellite campus, and asked if I could possibly take on a kind of substitute job for a course in Theatre that had rostered, but, at the moment, due to some emergency circumstances had no teacher. I was rather intrigued by the offer, and decided it would be interesting and challenging. I took the position, and enjoyed a very successful semester. When it was over, I was told by those in charge that they were pleased with what I had done, and would be interested in having me work for them again. However, I could not hope for full time work without a Master's degree.

I was content with things the way they were, and continued with my many pursuits.

Some months later, my father asked me if I would prepare a special dinner for friends he wanted to invite to our home. I told him I could certainly do that. On the night of the dinner, I met my father's guests: an engineering professor and, amazingly, the very woman from the Penn State faculty who had hired me to teach the course in drama at Penn State. We spent a lot of time talking over dinner, and by evening's end, the woman was encouraging me to get my Master's degree as she thought I would be a great addition to the local college faculty. After much thought, I decided to take a leave of absence from my high school teaching position, and pursue an advanced degree at SUNY University in Binghamton.

I did, in fact, earn my Master's in Theatre during that time and was able to keep up with my catering commitments. With the advanced degree, I was able to teach part time at Penn State's local satellite campus, and also became a member of the adjunct faculty at my alma mater Marywood College. I was also able to continue with my catering commitments and resume a position with the Catholic school system as an elementary teacher. During that same time, I did the necessary course work and gained permanent teaching certification in the system as well as credentials to work on the administrative level.

My plate was full, and I was enjoying a rich and satisfying multifaceted career.

ONE ENTRÉE AT A TIME

THE RICE STORY

Because I found myself shoulder high in catering jobs, I decided to convert the basement of my grandparents' home into a small catering kitchen. The basement already housed a refrigerator and several sinks. With the assistance of my grandparents, I purchased a small gas stove. As my grandfather was an excellent cook, converting the basement into a working kitchen was rather easy. He had used most of the basement as a canning cellar for fruits and vegetables. I remember many afternoons each September as I returned home from grade school, the savory smells that would waft from that canning cellar. I would walk up the driveway that led to our house and enjoy the smells of simmering tomatoes and chili sauce. It was canning season. Luckily for me, there were plenty of pots and pans left from those seasons as well as various cooking utensils that adorned the walls of this makeshift kitchen.

Throughout this time, on a full time level, I was still teaching school. Considering myself an educator, I also took on other part time endeavors to supplement my income. I taught a few classes on the college level, and still considered myself somewhat connected to local community theatre groups and their sporadic productions. In the midst of these many and varied pursuits, one day just before the Christmas holidays, the phone rang. Remember, at this time in my life, I still considered catering something of a hobby and one I had never really intended to pursue as a career. When I answered the phone, a woman on the other end inquired as to whether I would be available to cater a Christmas party for her and her husband the week before Christmas.

"How many guests?" I asked.

"About seventy five," she responded. My heart began to pound. I had never done a party for seventy five before.

For a split second I thought, "Can I handle this?" but without any noticeable hesitation I heard my own reply. "I would be happy to do your party." I could figure out the particulars later.

The woman had a simple menu in mind: some chicken with rice pilaf, Beef Bourguignon and a few other simple accompaniments including cold shrimp. I was sure I could handle that. I would get my fiancée Mary Ann to help me. She didn't really want to get involved in this business, but nevertheless was gracious enough to help me whenever I asked.

Joseph F. Caputo

I remember peeling shrimp past midnight on the night before the party. "Why am I doing this?" I asked her. "I must be crazy." Mary Ann was silent and just looked at me in amazement as we continued to peel the shrimp.

The next day I went to the local restaurant food store looking for rice packaged in large quantities. The only rice I ever cooked came out of a small box; up to this point I had never cooked for more than a dozen people.

I found a burlap bag of rice weighing about 10-15 pounds. "This should be enough," I said to myself. Better to have more than not enough.

That afternoon I packed the station wagon that my father had given me for the business. It was a real clunker, but it ran. I took one of my grandfather's huge canning pots. I figured it would be perfect for boiling the rice.

When I arrived at the site of the party, I immediately filled the huge pot with water and put it on the stove to boil. I knew it would take several hours.

Mary Ann came to help out as a waitress and she had also coerced one of her girlfriends to come along to help.

I had to stand up on a chair to gain access to the boiling pot of water. Without a moment of hesitation, I dumped the entire contents of the burlap bag of rice into the boiling pot. I put on the lid, lowered the heat on the stove and set the timer for thirty minutes.

I instructed the girls to use a slotted spoon to remove the rice and then put it into a chafing dish which I had prepared with some butter, chopped herbs and chicken broth. My recipes were very unsophisticated in those days. This was my rice pilaf. I told them that I had a back up of the seasoning mix and that periodically as they refilled the chafing dish throughout the night, they would need to add more of the tasty, well-seasoned concoction to the rice.

After hours of preparation and final presentation, the party was lauded as a great success. We had more than enough food, and everyone, especially the hostess, seemed very pleased with the evening.

As the girls and I continued to clean and pack the station wagon, I told them that I would take care of the pot we used for the rice as it was oversized and very heavy. To date, this party was the first party of such magnitude that I had catered, and I found myself very tired. I carefully stood up on the chair so that I could lift the pot off the stove. When I went to lift it, the pot was so heavy I couldn't budge it. "I can't be that tired," I thought. I lifted the lid and was shocked to see that the pot was full of rice!

"Girls," I exclaimed, "you forgot to serve the rice!"

"Joe, we've been filling the chafing dish with rice all night and adding that seasoning mix you gave us," Mary Ann protested.

"Yes," her girlfriend added. "I took rice out of that pot several times myself."

"It can't be," I retorted. The pot was almost full with rice. It must have just kept growing in the pot. I was confused since this was my first attempt to deal with such a large quantity of rice.

"Get me some plastic garbage bags," I ordered. The two came running with jumbo sized trash bags and I began to scoop the rice out of the pot with a slotted spoon. I put the rice into the garbage bag. The task seemed endless. When the pot was light enough and I was able to lift it from the stove, I dumped the remaining contents into another trash can liner. We had two half full bags in total. I did not completely fill one because I was afraid it would burst with the weight of the rice.

We dragged those bags like dead bodies across the kitchen floor and put the heavy bags outside where the trash cans were kept. They were too heavy to lift, so we just left them there alongside the trash cans.

As it turned out, the hostess had a set of silver teaspoons she wanted to use for the party as a display near the dessert table. I had advised her that I did not think it was a good idea to put the spoons out as people might think that they were to be used. Worse yet, there was the possibility of the heirloom spoons getting mixed in with the rental spoons we had for the party. In any case, I put out the spoons on the dessert table as the hostess had requested. I placed the twelve of them in a pretty fan arrangement alongside a demitasse cup and saucer that were also pieces from the estate of the hostess' grandmother.

The next day I received a phone call from the hostess informing me that the party was "lovely" and that everyone complimented the food and the service. I was very happy with the review. "However," she added, "I am missing one of my grandmother's teaspoons. Did you happen to see it?" she asked.

"No," I replied, "but I will call the rental company and see if the spoon got mixed in with theirs."

She was quick to add, "My husband and I even looked in the garbage outside!"

My next thought was that she would say, "And for the love of God....what was all that rice....?"

I was eager to end the call. "I'll call you if the spoon turns up," I assured her. "Thank you again for your business." I hung up the phone before she could get another word out.

And that's the rice story!

By the way, the spoon never did show up.

I want to include a rice recipe with this story.

For obvious reasons,

I have not chosen the rice pilaf dish from this particular event.

However, my grandmother did make a lovely baked rice dish that she would sometimes serve during the week with a green salad.

That recipe and other rice dishes can be found among the recipes in the Recipe Section.

THE PRIME RIB LOCK OUT

I have always had a lot of energy and wasn't really content unless I had a few irons in the fire. Not being a golfer or a runner, (unless I was trying to lose a few pounds), I preferred teaching a course here or there, performing in regional theatre, or singing at weddings. As my catering engagements increased, I felt up to the challenge even as I continued with my newly acquired full time position as principal in another Catholic school in the area.

One Christmas vacation, while serving as principal, I received a call from a woman who wanted to have a holiday party sometime between Christmas and New Year's Eve. This kind of arrangement always worked out perfectly for me. In fact, during those years, I only did parties during summer vacation, or during Christmas or Easter breaks. Once in a while, I might squeeze a party in on a weekend.

The woman insisted I meet with her at her home. The request was not unusual as most times I needed to scope out the kitchen and the dining area of a house so I could plan accordingly. During my visit, I would also arrange any rentals I might need for the party. The proposed party was going to be a nice holiday event for about 40 guests. The hostess had a very small dining room and so we decided to remove some of the furniture from the living room which was more or less connected to the dining room. I planned to rent some round tables which, when added to the existing dining room table, would comfortably seat 40 people.

The kitchen was adequate. The stove looked a bit dated, but overall everything was in good working order and the space would present no obstacles for a party this size. The hostess chose her menu with prime rib as the centerpiece of the dinner. She also wanted a Roasted Red Pepper Bisque which had become one of my trademark soups and to this day is the most requested soup in my repertoire.

The party was several weeks away. I had everything written down on paper and would be ready to rock and roll once we got out of school on December 23.

I ordered a substantial piece of prime rib of beef from a butcher who had ordered me great special cuts earlier. I would have to transport the meat. At that time I was driving a Honda Prelude, but I was sure I could fit the prime rib of beef for 40 people into the trunk since the piece would actually be cut into several pieces.

The day of the party arrived and I had decided to go to my client's house early in the morning because most of what I had to do for the dinner had to be done that day. As I knew her kitchen was adequate, I decided to do the lion's share of the work at her home. The soup was premade; the sides I would prep at her house, and, of course, the beef would have to slow roast for several hours in the oven at the woman's house. The hostess was so glad to see me when I arrived. She seemed calm and collected and that was always a good sign because I knew my client trusted me and would give me the license to do what had to be done.

"Well, I have some things to get done before the party," the hostess told me. "If you need anything. . ." and then she stopped. "Oh, by the way," she added, "the oven isn't working today; I don't know why."

"That could be a problem." What an understatement! I had over two hundred dollars' worth of prime rib sitting in the car. Thank God, it was December and cold enough to safely keep the meat in the car until I was ready for it. "Let me take a look at the oven," I said as I moved toward the stove which looked vintage circa 1975. I turned on the oven. Nothing! No lights. Nothing happened. I began to turn on the burners; they worked and began to heat up. "Well," I said, "it's early enough in the day to call my friend at the rental company and get a stove up here. We can put it in the garage."

"Oh, we can't do that," she protested. "My husband said that the electricity in the garage isn't working and there is no way that he can fix it today."

Her husband wasn't even home. How did she know all this? How did he know I would need electricity in the garage? I was not about to argue as time was wasting. Furthermore, when I pressed the hostess about when her husband would return, she said, "around" dinnertime. He was a city policeman and his hours were always uncertain. After I heard that, I was convinced that I shouldn't argue about the electricity situation in the house. I put on my chef coat and walked toward the front door of the house.

"Where are you going?" she asked.

"I'm going to start knocking on the doors of your neighbors' houses," I replied.

"We just moved into the neighborhood a few months ago; we really don't know anyone here," she added.

"Look," I insisted, "I need a stove; just do what you have to do, and I will do what I have to do in order to cook that meat!" I exited the door before she had a chance to say anything more."

There was a large stone house located just diagonally across the street. "Good place to start," I thought. A huge home like that had to have a large oven, if not two. Adjusting my chef coat and taking a deep breath, I rang the doorbell. A middle aged woman answered the door and seemed quite surprised by my professional appearance.

"Are you from the Food Network?" she asked.

"No," I responded, "Not yet. Do you know your neighbors over there across the street?" I asked, pointing toward the house across the way and in full view.

"No," the woman quickly responded. "I'm afraid I haven't had the opportunity to meet them."

"Well, tonight may be the time to do just that," I suggested. "Is your husband at home?"

"Oh no," she replied. "I was recently divorced."

"I'm sorry," I said. "Maybe tonight will be your lucky night for meeting someone new." The woman was now very confused.

"What do you mean?" she asked.

I answered with a bold announcement. "It just so happens that your neighbors are having a lovely dinner party tonight and you're invited."

"Invited?" she asked. "Me?"

"Yes," I responded. "Do you have a nice party dress?"

"I think I do."

"Well, great," I continued. "Dinner is being served around 6 p.m. I do hope you will join us."

"Maybe I will," she said.

"There's just one favor I need to ask of you," I quickly added.

"What's that?" she asked.

"I need your oven; do you have an oven?"

She looked at me almost as if I came from another planet. "Of course, I have an oven," she said.

"May I come in?" I asked, moving toward the inside of the house before she had a chance to invite me in. "Oh, this is so lovely," I began to exclaim as I worked my way toward the interior of the house and the kitchen. The woman moved in right behind me and the next thing we knew, the two of us were standing in a very modern and well appointed kitchen. I spied not one, but two Jen Air ovens right in the wall. "These are great ovens. Will I be able to use them?" I asked.

"Of course," was the response, but the woman looked totally confused and I began to explain.

"You see, your neighbor's oven is not working and I asked the hostess if she knew you since you live just across the street. When the hostess told me she had not had the opportunity to meet you, I figured now was the perfect time. You come to the party and meet the neighbors and I'll use your oven to cook the dinner."

"Oh," she said as she sorted things out. "That sounds like the perfect plan."

"It is," I announced gleefully as I opened the oven door of the top unit to check out its interior. "Look, I'm going to go over and get the prime rib, season it up and bring it back over here to roast. I can put one roast in the bottom oven and one in the top. Is that ok?"

"Why, of course." The bargain was made!

I quickly said my goodbyes and made my way over to the other house so I could season up the meat, return to the other house and get it in the oven. The party was still about five hours away; I felt I had plenty of time.

When I returned with the seasoned prime ribs, I put one in the top oven and one in the bottom just as I had planned. I inserted a probe meat thermometer into the smaller sized rib as I knew this one would be ready to eat first. I could judge about how much longer to leave the second roast in the oven until it was cooked medium. "When this alarm goes off, dial this number." As this was a time before the dawn of the cell phone, I handed the woman a piece of paper on which the phone number of her neighbor was printed. She couldn't have been more gracious. "I'll call you as soon as it goes off," she said.

"Thanks, and don't forget to get ready for the party at 6!" I called back as I made my way out of the kitchen.

I got back to the neighbor's house and began to busy myself with other items that had to be prepared.

I put the fresh butternut squash ravioli in the freezer. The salad greens were washed and wrapped in paper towels. I put them in the vegetable bin of the refrigerator. My back up help would be arriving in about another hour. I wanted to be sure that I had everything ready so we could get this party up and running.

Margaret and I at the stove ready for action

When my back up crew did arrive, I announced to Margaret, a longtime friend who had graciously agreed to help me, that we would be expecting a phone call when the beef was ready. She and I would retrieve the meat from across the street while the other workers carried on with the first two courses of the meal. I had arranged for one of my waiters to pick up a heat lamp that I kept in my garage at home. I would turn on the heat lamp and keep the cooked prime rib warm and resting under the glow of the infrared lights. I was ready.

The first course was served. The Roasted Red Pepper Bisque received rave reviews according to my tuxedo clad waiters. "Joe, they love it!" one of my waiters announced in the kitchen.

"That's great," but I was distracted and waiting for that phone to ring. We still had the salad course to go and the butternut squash ravioli with sage brown butter.

As the chilled plates were being filled with the crisp greens dressed with my orange vinaigrette dressing, the phone on the wall began to ring. "It's the meat!" I exclaimed. "Give me that phone!" Now I was shouting.

"Hello, hello!" I must have been yelling because a chorus of "shhhhhhhhs" resounded throughout the kitchen.

"The alarm is ringing," a calm voice reported on the other end of the line.

"Oh, thank you." Now, I was whispering "I'll be right over." I grabbed my coat and told Margaret to do the same. "It's time," I announced. The two of us discreetly exited the front door of the house. We had to pass through the hallway and luckily we were on the fringes of the larger area of the living room where the tables filled with guests ready for the second course were chatting and laughing. No one noticed that the chef was exiting the house!

We crossed the snow laden streets as it had been snowing for some time. It really looked pretty, so clean and white. The newly fallen snow was settling gently on the lawn that had been covered with dirty snow from the last snowfall.

When I arrived at the neighbor's house, my "mustered assistant" was dressed in a pretty yet simple party dress. "Oh you look great," I announced. "So festive!"

Joseph F. Caputo

"Thank you, I thought I would join the party for dessert, if that's OK with you."

"Whatever you like," I responded.

"I have to go out on an errand, but I'll be back in about an hour and then I'll come over," she said.

"Great!" I said.

"I'll be on my way and lock up right after you leave," she said.

"That will be fine and, oh, by the way, meet one of my helpers. This is Margaret. I'm not sure I ever got your name," I said to the woman.

"It's Judy."

"Margaret, this is Judy," I said as I began to open the ovens and see the beauty of the roasts inside. I probed the larger one with the instant read thermometer I had stashed in my coat pocket. It would be fine just as it was. "You better be careful driving, Judy," I added. "It's beginning to snow."

"Oh, thank you. Do you need help?" she offered.

"I don't think so," I replied. "Margaret can handle the smaller pan and I will take the larger." We carefully lifted the roasting pans from the oven with the aid of some kitchen towels. I tented them with some foil I had taken with me. Margaret took the smaller roast and I took the heavier. "See you later, Judy," I said as we all left the house together.

Margaret and I began our trek back across the street and down the snow covered walk. Since the house was diagonally across the street, we had to walk a bit on the sidewalk before we could make our way up the front walk and then the front steps of the house. Then it dawned on me. How could we make a subtle entrance using the front door? "It might be better to go around the back," I said to Margaret.

The two of us began to cross the front lawn with the steaming roasting pans. As we approached the driveway that led to the back of the house, we discovered that a gate that separated the front yard and rear deck areas of the house was locked. "We're going to have to go through the front," I said to Margaret. "We can't get through here."

Resembling two cartoon character silhouettes that were sneaking around carrying pans of roasted meat, the two of us retraced our steps through the snowy lawn.

We trekked our way up the front steps and I reached for the door while trying to balance the hot roasting pan I was carrying. Leaning my bodyweight against the pan to hold it in place against the door, I grabbed for the door knob. "The door is locked!" I exclaimed. "It's locked! Now what?"

We had no cell phones to call anyone in the house. The only cell phones that were on the market at the time were cumbersome bag phones. Judy had gone on her errand and would not be back for an hour. I had several hundred dollars worth of roasted prime rib that was quickly cooling down. It was getting dark, and I was locked out of the house for the very dinner party I was catering.

"I can't ring the doorbell," I said. I knew the ringing would draw too much attention to the door. I was trying to be discreet. Pizza gets delivered, not prime rib!

"Let's go back around the other side. Maybe I can unlatch that gate that leads to the back deck."

"OK," answered Margaret, who I could tell by now was cold and getting tired from holding the pan. Her pan was smaller than the one I was holding, but it still had a substantially large prime rib snuggled inside it.

As we began to trace our steps for a third time over the snow covered lawn, we could hear the garage door, not far from view, begin to open. "We're saved," I announced. Someone was coming out of the garage and was carrying what looked like a snare drum. "Can you hold that door?" I shouted.

It was the hostess' son. He was loading his car with drums as he was in a rock band and about to depart for his gig. "Please, hold that door," I yelled again. The young man looked astonished as he saw us—silhouetted characters carrying steaming roasting pans over his front lawn.

"We got locked out," I explained, and quickly added, "Thanks." He still looked dazed as he retrieved another drum and went about his packing.

Once inside the garage, I looked for the entrance to the house. I had no idea where that entrance would lead. I hoped somewhere close to the kitchen. After I had managed to climb the half dozen steps that led into the house, with Margaret close at hand, I was relieved when I opened the door to find that I was, in fact, in the kitchen. The staff looked at me in amazement. "Quick!" I commanded. "Get these pans and get them under the heat lamp."

I quickly took off my coat and began to inspect the meat inside the pans. "Let's get them out of these pans and wrapped in foil." I was in full command mode. Once wrapped in the foil and placed under the heat lamps the meat would be perfect for serving after the pasta course.

We retrieved the tender ravioli from the boiling pot of water, and then ladled a generous amount of sage brown butter atop each bowl. I finished the dish with a grating of fresh parmesan and a deep fried sage leaf. It was perfection!

The rest of the dinner went without a hitch. The prime rib was perfect and the guests were raving about the marvelous meal.

Judy did show up for dessert, and, of course, I introduced her as the neighbor next door who happened to drop in. Everyone was sworn to secrecy on the beef escapade.

TAKE IT OFF: EPISODE ONE

When the Prime Rib party finally ended after a long evening, the guests all left, happy and full.

My wife Mary Ann had come to join me at the end of the night because I was afraid I did not have enough room in my small Honda to take all of the things I had used for the party back to my garage and basement.

My wife's car was a bit larger and had a roomy trunk and back seat. One trip was all I intended as the weather forecast for the next day projected more snow and icy road conditions.

It was about 2 a.m. by the time we packed up our cars. I had instructed my wife that we would take a back road home. The snow was light and the back road proved to be a shorter route to our house than going on the highway.

Mary Ann protested about the back road, "Someone was murdered there once, remember?"

"Yes," I replied while I thought it was probably a drug deal that had gone bad ten years ago. "No need to worry," I announced. "You lead the way and I'll be directly behind you." After some protest, she finally agreed.

It was late and the two of us were tired and anxious to get home.

My wife pulled out of the driveway first and drove down the street toward the back road we planned to take as the short cut home. I slowly backed my car out of the driveway in pursuit. Suddenly, I saw the hostess running out of the house and flailing her arms in midair as she called my name. "Joseph, Joseph!" she yelled.

I stopped the car abruptly. By now my wife was driving down the street just a few blocks away from the road where once "someone had been murdered."

I rolled down my window and asked, "What is it? Did I forget something?"

"Oh no," she replied.

She continued to explain that she was alone in the house. I remembered that her husband had left the party earlier to go back to his beat. She filled me in with other details. Her son, who I knew was gone on his rock band gig, would not be back until the wee hours of the morning.

"And," I asked myself, "where is this leading?" Yet, I remained silent as she continued to ramble.

"I thought I'd cut myself out," she said. "But it was so expensive."

Because of so many culinary challenges at the prime rib dinner party, I forgot to mention what turned out to be a rather interesting fact. The hostess was dressed in a leather dress that was more reminiscent of a cat suit than a dress. She wore it well, despite the fact that it was very tight. And there she was, trying her best to make me understand her dilemma. Slowly, it dawned on me; she couldn't get out of the. . . cat suit!

"Would you mind unzipping me?" she asked somewhat timidly.

I could hardly speak. It was 2 a.m. on a cold December night. A woman in a black leather cat dress was standing in her driveway. Her husband was a policeman. I had just had an ordeal with a prime rib that almost didn't make it to the dinner table. Now what? "Ok," I said. At this point in my career I was still the principal in a Catholic school, and caution was my middle name. "I'll do it as long as we do it right here in the driveway."

I opened my car door and got out. She turned around. With one decisive zip, I undid the entire zipper of the dress.

Half falling out of her stilettos and laughing like a school girl, the policeman's wife ran up her snow covered walkway and into her house.

I got back in my car, not laughing, turned up the heat and rolled up the window. A second dawning was upon me—-my wife Mary Ann was on murderer's row by now and I hadn't even left the driveway!

I drove as quickly as road conditions would allow. The back road that led to the shortest distance home was even darker than I imagined. The new fallen snow lay gently on the branches of the tall trees that lined each side of the road. Just a few more miles and I would be home. Mary Ann's car was nowhere in sight.

As I turned onto the street where we lived, I could see that every light in our house was illuminated, even the front porch and walkways. "That is never a good sign," I thought. Most times if I came home late from a party, my wife would leave a light on outside and maybe one in the main hall of the house.

With the house fully illuminated, I knew she hadn't gone to bed, but was wondering where in God's name I could be. She was either worrying herself to death or growing more and more angry.

When I finally did manage to get myself into the house, I was greeted with a barrage of near hysterical remarks, "You said you would be right behind me. What happened? Where were you? That road was so dark and you were not behind me! Where were you?"

"You better sit down," I began, and slowly continued. "You know how on the new '*Catering by Joseph*' business card, it reads-"from start to finish?"

"Yes," she responded, not sure where this was going.

"Well tonight I really finished it," and I explained to my wife exactly what had happened. Plain and simple!

"Thank God, you didn't go into the house," she said as I finished the story.

"Give me some credit," I said with a hint of panache. "That thought never occurred to me!"

HALF BEEF WILL TRAVEL

During my last year as principal, the high school that I had graduated from was preparing for its 40th reunion. It was the school itself, mind you, not my class, that had been in existence for forty years. I was contacted about catering that event. Actually I was enamored of my alma mater, very happy to be part of the festivities, and honored to be selected for what so many of us considered a prestigious event. The party was set for May and by that time I knew in the back of my mind that this might be my very last year as principal. I decided to take the catering job as it might just be the beginning of the "all new" catering business. The committee suggested that I do a steamship of beef as one of the food stations for the party. I had never cooked a steamship of beef.

Months before the reunion, I had to go to Boston for a convention of educators where I would represent the school. While at the convention, I attended a beautiful cocktail party hosted by the uniform company from which our school purchased uniforms for many years. To my delight, one of the food stations was a steamship of beef. The chef who was carving the steaming mound of flavor looked austere, yet at the same time proud of his accomplishment. "Did you cook that?" I asked.

"Yes," he simply replied.

"How long?" I continued.

"Seven hours," he responded.

"What temperature?" I pressed.

"325 degrees."

I had my recipe. Bring on the beef!

Once I returned home, I called my butcher and told him to order me a steamship of beef. I was instructed that the beef would be in on Friday. That was perfect, I thought; the party was slated for Saturday. After school on Friday afternoon, I drove to the butcher shop and anxiously went inside to purchase my steamship of beef.

I had placed an order for the meat I wanted, and the butcher had the meat ready when I arrived. I paid him as I stared incredulously at the huge piece of meat that sat in the meat locker.

"Where's your truck?" he asked.

"Truck? What truck?" I could barely get the words out. My small Honda Prelude could only hold so much, and though it had served me well, I thought this particular piece of meat was way over the top as cargo. I went out to the parking lot and drove my small sports car up to the main door of the shop. The butcher and I managed to get the humongous piece of meat, heavily wrapped in plastic, into the front bucket seat, where we secured it by strapping it in with the seat belt.

"How long do I have?" I asked. As the weather was quite temperate, he instructed me that I had only about two hours to get the meat into a cooler.

Since I had some time, I decided to drive to my house and show my wife the beautiful piece of meat I had purchased for our high school's anniversary party. I pulled up to the front of my house and proudly began to beep the horn. My wife stuck her head out the front door and asked, "Who's in the car with you?"

"It's the beef!" I exclaimed.

She looked at me in disbelief. "I thought it was a person!" she retorted. From that point on, the steamship was known as "Elsie."

I brought the meat to the high school and went to the cafeteria where I put it into the cooler. Thank heavens, the cooler there was big enough. I cooked the meat just as my chef mentor from Boston had instructed. The reunion was a great success and "Elsie" was the star of the show.

FALLING "INTO THE SOUP"

I continued to book a few parties here and there to the degree my schedule would permit, but my income still came primarily from my position as a principal. What had begun to happen, however, was that my invitations to orchestrate small dinner parties were on the incline while the future of the educational system I was part of seemed to be heading toward a rapid decline and possible ending. I decided to proceed with great caution. I wanted to keep all my options open. Yet, in all honesty, I was finding myself more attracted to pursuing the kinds of experiences I was having in the catering business than those in a position that was becoming less and less viable.

In June of 2004, the pastor of the parish which supported the grade school showed up in my office. With no fanfare, he simply said he had come to inform me that I would not be returning as the principal in the fall. In spite of all my earlier misgivings about the permanence of my position, I can honestly say I was shocked. I left the building after lunch that day and decided I needed to go for a ride to sort things out.

I got into my car, and less than two hours later, I drove into the parking lot of the *Culinary Institute of America* in Hyde Park, New York. This was my second excursion to the *CIA*.

Ironically, just the year before, one of the fifth grade teachers had invited me to chaperone a field trip to the *Culinary Institute of America*. I remember saying, "Of course, I would love to go!"

The *CIA* trip interested me. As always, in the back of my mind, but still a remote possibility at that time, I thought that I might one day broaden my involvement on the culinary stage. That trip to the *CIA* was very satisfying, not just for the students but for me as well. I took the opportunity to speak to a few admissions counselors at the Institute who informed me that there were food enthusiasts programs and other professional development classes that might be of interest to me if I ever chose to pursue culinary. I spent some time familiarizing myself with the very impressive facility.

With those memories in mind, and with the knowledge that I was not returning to my position as principal in the upcoming fall, I had serious decisions to make. If, indeed, I could not be assured of being rehired for the fall term in a different capacity within the educational system, what was I waiting for?

When I arrived at the *CIA* on that June afternoon, I went directly to the registrar's office of continuing education and signed up for a Culinary Boot Camp that would begin in September. This would be the first time in so many years that I would be returning to school, not as a teacher or a principal, but as a student. It was a new beginning. I wrote out the check; tucked the receipt in my wallet and left the building. I bought a sandwich at the snack bar in the student center. I walked down as close to the shore of the Hudson River that the pathway near the school allowed. I sat down and I calmly ate my sandwich.

My cell phone broke the silence, and then my "Hello."

"Where are you?" A voice on the other end of the phone asked. It was my wife Mary Ann.

"I'm near the Hudson River," I responded.

"What?" And before I had a chance to say anything she asked, "Please don't tell me you're thinking about going back to school?"

"I'll be home in a couple of hours," I responded, "and then I'll explain everything."

When the call ended, I finished my sandwich, walked back to my car and began the drive home.

A change was imminent. Expediency had given me the courage to make a life changing decision. I was ready to acknowledge the satisfaction and pleasure that preparing food was giving me and the contentment that had grown within me for quite some time. I was also quite sure that my years as an administrator were behind me. I was geared for a new future.

That September I took the basic training class and enjoyed the experience. I will never forget the night before school was about to begin. I drove to Hyde Park early on Sunday evening. Classes were to begin the following day. I was filled with trepidation as I drove over the Newburgh bridge that crossed the Hudson. This would be the first time in a long time that I would be a student. Not just any student, but a culinary student! Who would I meet and how would I succeed in a new venture that I felt I knew much about, but professionally had no credentials for?

I checked into a motel near the school and went to bed early since I had to be in class, dressed in uniform by 7 a.m. Next morning, I awoke at 6 a.m. I showered and, for the first time, I put on my chef pants, chef coat, neck handkerchief and chef clogs. I took one look in the mirror and thought I would heave the coffee that I had made and drank earlier, thanks to a complimentary coffee service bar.

"This is nuts!" I thought. "I must be crazy." I looked silly. Another costume? Another show?

Yet, deep down I knew I was doing the right thing. I knew that despite the awkwardness of the moment, I *was* in the right place and it *was* the right time. I moved into my day, and many other days thereafter.

I loved the training so much that during the following winter, I took four more Saturday classes. One of those classes was Soups. I also returned to the *CIA* for additional classes in French and Italian cuisine during the following two summers.

With my honed skills, I began moving from thinking about to moving into some serious action. I followed a similar pattern as the one I had followed years before when I revamped my grandfather's kitchen. At home, I found a small kitchen that was for rent in a garage located in a small court near the city. The woman who owned the garage had a soup business and decided she wanted out. I had heard about the kitchen through a friend. When I first saw the facility, I wasn't sure what I wanted to do. I knew I could get a license from the city. I also knew that the kitchen, though small, was adequate. It had a commercial stove, a grill, a griddle, a three bay sink, and a walk in cooler and freezer. The area had everything I needed, but the kitchen, only as big as my bedroom, could be something of a challenge.

I told the woman who wanted to rent it out that I would think about it. The rent was reasonable, but up to this point, I was officially unemployed. "Catering by Joseph" was, in my mind, a hobby, something I did on vacation or for a few weekends a year. Without a steady job, I didn't know how I could afford to rent the kitchen and keep my house, my car and every other expense in tow.

Until I could get the business built, I thought I might collect partial unemployment, continue my adjunct work at the university and work part time in my new venture. That prospect looked bleak. I had a mortgage, a car payment, and I had to help my wife with whatever other house expenses that her salary could not cover at the time. I wasn't sure what I was going to do. I did file for unemployment benefits.

Only a few days later, the phone rang. A gentleman on the phone informed me that he had heard that I was renting the kitchen from the woman who used to make soup for his "ready to eat foods" market. "She made the best soup." He sounded so sincere, and then continued. "Can you make soup?"

"Yes, I can make soup," I responded.

I had made soup only at home. But I did some soup making in culinary school and had taken a special class there in the art of soup making. Also, I had a long standing love affair with soups.

My mother loved to travel; my father did not. So many times, along with Mary Ann, the girl I was dating and later married, I would travel with my mother to all the places she loved to visit. My wife and I share fond memories of our trips with Mom to the Bahamas, St. Marten, Aruba, Acapulco, Cancun, and Miami. One year we finally convinced my dad to join us on a trip to Cape Cod and Nantucket. He must have had a good time because the following year he joined us on a cruise to St. Thomas, San Juan and Labadee, Haiti. Of course, on all of those trips, my mother insisted we eat our way through the best restaurants each place had to offer.

From the conch chowder in the Caribbean to the creamy white clam chowder of New England, these experiences were shaping my culinary point of view without my even knowing it. I was exposed to many different types of foods and, in most cases, on my return home, I would try to reproduce any dish we had enjoyed on vacation, especially the soups!

French Onion Soup was one of the best soups I had ever eaten. I remembered that there was a lovely little place in New York City called "La Potagerie." The restaurant was located on Fifth Avenue and I had gone there many times with my friends and my mother when I lived in the city and even after I returned home. We would always laugh and say "twenty bowls" as we ran down Fifth Avenue toward the eatery on our many visits.

Beginning at noon, the restaurant claimed to have only twenty bowls of French Onion soup in addition to the other soup choices for the day. The soup, along with a piece of aged cheddar, an apple and a piece of French baguette, was a complete meal for less than ten dollars. It made for a great and inexpensive lunch.

I loved soup and obviously still do. Once again, I had no clue that these adventures would eventually help lead me to a career in the kitchen, one in the catering business and one as a soup chef.

What did this man mean when he asked me, "Can you make soup?" And what part of my psyche responded with undeniable certainty, "Yes, I can make soup"?

"How much soup do you need?" I asked.

"About ten gallons a week," was his response. I began to do the math in my head: ten gallons of soup per week times four weeks. I added the total to a rounded out figure of what I expected to earn with my additional catering and, "I'll make it," came tumbling out of my mouth without another moment's hesitation.

"Good! It's Wednesday, I need ten gallons of Roasted Red Pepper Bisque on Friday."

"You'll have it!"

And with that, my soup business started. Just like that! Preparing it in that kitchen in the alley, I made soup for that man for years, and continued my catering service.

TO ZUPPA

I began with an order for ten gallons of soup. Three years later, I was making 90 gallons a week. However, I was still working in a very small kitchen in an alley. On the upside, the catering business had grown somewhat, and the soup business was going through the ceiling. I never did collect on the claim I had filed for unemployment.

I continued to work in that same kitchen which was not only small, but also remote, quiet, and isolated. Some days were lonely. Most days I worked alone. Some days I got a friend or two to help. It wasn't easy. The equipment was adequate but most was worn. On several occasions, the cooler or freezer would break down. I lost food a few times. I lost money. I had to freeze garbage since pick up was scheduled only once a week. Then there was the smell of food cooking. Although I had a license with the city, I was working in a garage that had been converted into a kitchen in a residential section. I didn't want any of the neighbors complaining.

I had limited parking and it was hard to load in provisions, sometimes very late at night—- always in the very small area of the alley. It was also difficult to load out parties because many times cars were parked right in front of the door that led to the kitchen.

I remember on several occasions, cleaning out the freezer after it had broken down. I would be on my hands and knees scrubbing the freezer floor and asking myself *and* God, just how long I would have to stay in a secluded alley making soup. I loved to cook, but here again, I had to find a way to let my business grow and prosper. As for myself, I had to move into a location where I could really blossom as a chef.

For three solid years, I made soup and catered parties. Sometimes, from that kitchen in the alley, I did weddings or events for several hundred people. There were lighter moments too, and one of those had to do, not with soup, but with a salad dressing I had created. It caused quite a reaction.

THE SALAD DRESSING DEAL

"This is sooooooo delicious."

"You should bottle this."

"Can I buy some of this?"

It seemed that after every cooking demo I did or every party where I served my signature salad with the orange vinaigrette, people couldn't stop telling me how marvelous the dressing was.

The funny thing is that of all the dishes, soups, sauces and other things I cooked and concocted on a daily basis, making the dressing was my least favorite chore. It still is. I just dislike making it, but people love it.

Although I heard constant acclaim for the dressing, for years, it didn't dawn on me that I should, in fact, bottle the dressing. That in itself is a story, but the dressing is now bottled and can be purchased.

Before the golden goodness was put into a bottle, I would make it quart after quart, for sale, gallon after gallon for the restaurant.

One afternoon I received a call from a woman who wanted to buy three quarts of the Orange Vinaigrette. This happened before I had opened my restaurant Zuppa, and I really had an aversion to having people come to a garage where I had my small catering kitchen which I used to prepare most of the food for the parties I catered. The kitchen was very small. It was located in an alley, and there was no room for parking.

When the woman who wanted the dressing told me where she lived, I told her that I could meet her halfway in the parking lot of a nearby restaurant. It was only a ten minute drive for both of us so it seemed the perfect arrangement.

As I painstakingly mixed the dressing, I decided to make a few extra quarts and take them with me.

You just never know. Customers have been known to request a certain number of anything and then once they see it, they place additional orders.

I packed up about 12 quarts of the dressing in my SUV and I drove off to the designated spot where I would meet my customer.

The woman arrived right on time. I opened the hatchback of my car and retrieved the three quarts of dressing. It was a cash exchange. At that moment, like lightning, the thought suddenly struck me, "Is this legal?"

Now that I am involved in a corporation and a restaurant that is a division of that company, I am rigidly cautious about any financial transactions. At that time, however, I was so naïve that selling a few quarts of salad dressing for less than $20 was not really something I thought twice about.

As the woman was paying me for the dressing, several other people were leaving the restaurant just yards away from us. "What is that?" a young woman asked. "Orange vinaigrette dressing," I innocently replied.

"Do you have any more for sale?" she asked.

"Yes, I do." The truth is I had nine other quarts.

"I'll take two." She was quite resolute. Before I had finished the transaction with her, more people were exiting the restaurant and came over to see what was for sale. I had a salad dressing operation going on. "It's like a drug deal," I thought, "selling out of the trunk of my car."

I sold all twelve containers in about ten minutes.

Needless to say, I never did that again, but don't think that before the dressing appeared in a professionally prepared bottle, with all the guidelines that such a product entailed, that the thought of selling out of my trunk never did tempt me again.

In August 2010, I arranged for the production of my dressing

Joseph's Citrus Orange Vinaigrette

with a co-packer in New Haven, Connecticut.

The bottled dressing is available at Zuppa and other retail stores in Scranton.

www.soupsforyou.com.

COOLING OFF FROM THE HEAT OF THE KITCHEN

Some days, I was working twelve or more hours in my little kitchen in the alley. I was working harder than I had ever worked in my life. I loved it, but, after a while, I felt I needed a vacation. During the summer of that third year, my wife Mary Ann and I decided to take a cruise to Alaska. I did still teach part time at the university. The soup business was good and the catering business filled in many financial gaps.

We took the trip to Alaska with six of our friends. The ship left from the port of Seattle. On the morning of the sailing, we were meandering through the streets of Seattle. We stopped in a shop for some coffee. I was getting antsy and I told Mary Ann I would meet the crowd back at the hotel before we departed for the port later that afternoon. I wanted some time to walk around and walk off my usual pre-vacation jitters.

I found a small interior mall in the city and went inside. I spotted a huge sign on a rather small eating establishment. The sign read "SOUP." Of course I was interested, so I went inside the restaurant.

A middle aged man who seemed to be the owner of the restaurant was stirring one of about six or eight steaming kettles of soup set up behind the glass of a serving counter.

"What do you have there?" I asked.

"Soup," he answered.

"What kind?" I asked.

"This is crab bisque and all the others are listed up there on the wall," he answered.

"Is that all you serve here? Soup?" I asked.

"We have some salads and sandwiches as well," was his brief response. I picked up a takeout menu, wished him a good day and left the restaurant to go back to the hotel.

That night as Mary Ann and I, along with our friends, dined on the high seas, I raised my glass and announced a toast, "To *ZUPPA!*" I said.

"Zuppa?" My wife was puzzled.

"Zuppa?" Our friends were equally puzzled.

"Yes, Zuppa," I repeated. It means soup in Italian. A round of "Oh's" could be heard round the table, but by the expressions on my friends' faces and especially the one on my wife's face, who gave me that "He's crazy!" look, I knew I had more explaining to do.

"*Zuppa*" is the name of my new restaurant, the one I'm going to open when we go home."

Enough said. Each night of the cruise we'd raise our glasses and make what became a familiar toast "To *Zuppa!*"

A DREAM REALIZED

By the time we returned from our trip, it was late June. I began to get cold feet. Could I really make this work? Could I actually have a place of my own, with a well equipped kitchen for a luncheonette, and tables and chairs for eager patrons looking for a satisfying and delicious lunch? I knew I had to try.

I found a space for rent in a professional complex, very close to, but outside of the center of town. When I got there, the door to the space was unlocked. I walked in and peered at a dirt floor and four cinderblock walls. I took a deep breath and said a silent prayer. Then I called the owner of the building, and told him I wanted to rent the facility.

I gave my notice to the woman from whom I had been renting the kitchen in the alley. I told her that I would be vacating in December. I felt free, and ready to move forward. In August, I signed a lease with the landlord of the complex. With some reluctance, I stopped making soup the following January for the gentleman who owned the "ready to eat" foods store. He was devastated. I had toyed with the idea of making the soup for him and for me, but I wanted my soup to be exclusive and only available at my new restaurant "*Zuppa*."

It was about this same time that I had another gentle reminder to follow my dreams.

I needed to buy some piece of restaurant equipment, and went to a local restaurant supply store. A gentleman there told me that he didn't have whatever I needed, but that I should check another supply store in town. I was tired and decided to just go home.

But the next day, I decided to go to the other store. I don't know why. I had already decided that I didn't really need whatever I had been shopping for the day before. Still, I felt compelled to go to the other store that had been recommended.

When I arrived, I began to look around as I had never been there before. It was like a restaurant owner's *candy store*. This place had it all.

While I went from one thing to another, I heard a voice call, "Hey, cuz!" I turned and standing there was my cousin Steve, a man I hadn't seen in over 20 years.

"What are you doing here?" I asked.

"I own this place. What are *you* doing here?"

"I'm about to open a restaurant," and it seemed that after so many years, we were destined to meet.

It certainly was a fortunate meeting for the both of us: two cousins who had not seen each other for a lot of years, and now each of us was a business opportunity for the other.

Yet to me, that chance meeting meant so much more.

Steve and I arranged a meeting to talk over my new restaurant, and what I would need. He also offered to help me in any way he could. Without his guidance and expertise, the task of setting up a restaurant would have been much more difficult, if not impossible for me.

When the meeting was over, and I got into my car, I began to cry. Now, my dream of opening a restaurant was going to be realized. Steve was going to give me a break on all the equipment I needed, and he was also eager to advise me and give me other tips for making solid plans. For me, these details, great as they were, were secondary. I thought back to my childhood. Steve's mom and my mother were first cousins. My sister and I called Steve's mom whose name was Sadie, Aunt Sadie, out of love and respect.

Countless Sunday afternoons, I spent with Aunt Sadie, my grandmother and my mother. Aunt Sadie made visits to our house every Sunday afternoon for as long as I can remember. I always ran to the kitchen with my grandmother to put on the coffee and, of course, cut the cake or plate the biscotti or whatever else my grandmother had lovingly made that morning in anticipation of Aunt Sadie's visit.

My mom always smiling, giving, loving- even now from above!

I knew then as now that my meeting with Steve was not an accident. And though our mothers had since passed, I knew that they were still at work, helping each of us to fulfill our dreams.

Steve worked diligently with my sister Rosemary's husband, who is also named Steve. The two of them came up with a design. My brother-in-law Steve was project manager and my cousin Steve consulted on the kitchen. My brother-in-law who is really a "jack of all trades" saved me thousands of dollars as he was able to build the cabinetry as well as do some of the more detailed electrical work I had planned for the restaurant. Without his talent, skilled hands and direction, my dream would never have been realized.

The project took an amazing five months.

That February "*Zuppa*" opened its doors. During that same week, "The Soup Man" of Seinfeld fame opened a restaurant in town as well. The opening of a national competitor never upset me. I stayed true to who and what I was and still am today.

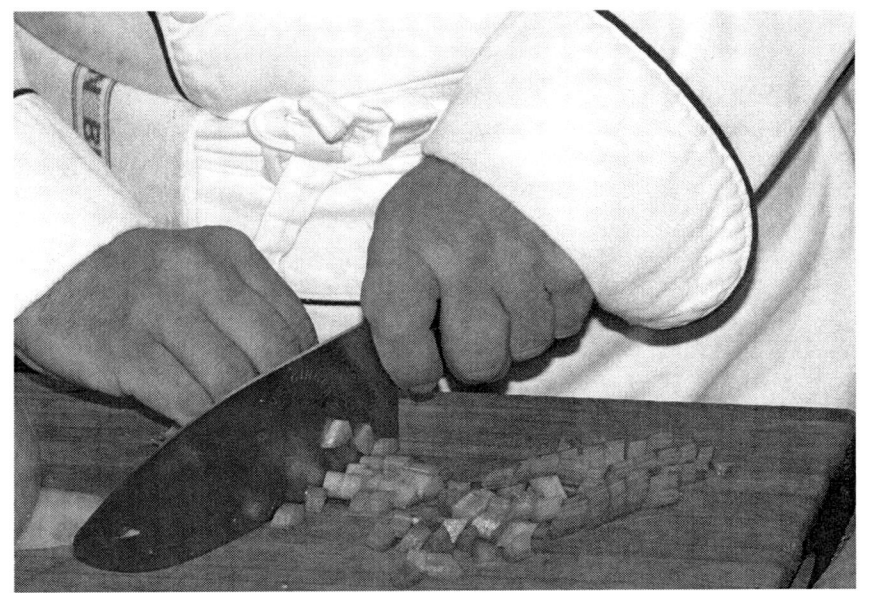

I offered premium soup in larger portions at a more reasonable price. One year later "The Soup Man" closed its doors. In fact, the restaurant supply company that special ordered "Soup Man's" spoons, sold me its surplus for next to nothing. I was going to hang one of those spoons in a frame on the wall, but after much thinking I decided to take a more humble approach and guided by the philosophy I had long before adopted, just continue to make the best soup I could.

As our menu states, "Soups from the heart and soul to warm and comfort....Influenced at a young age by my mother and her parents, our soup recipes reflect their inspiration, their love and the labor of their gifted hands. We craft our soups by hand with a knife, using only the freshest quality ingredients and present them to you for your enjoyment with that same love and sense of family pride.

Mangia!"

JOE VERSES THE VOLCANO

The Tripp House

The Tripp House in Scranton, Pennsylvania, is the oldest residence in Lackawanna County. The house was built circa 1778 by early New England settlers and is registered as a National Historic site. The house was taken over by a group of interested backers who turned the structure into a catering facility. They were able to maintain the property and the house without compromising the historical integrity of the building. It remains a popular site for all types of celebrations.

One evening, I catered a high school reunion for a group of senior aged women who were mostly widows. In fact, one of the women who arranged the reunion sat on the board of the Society for the Preservation of the Tripp Family Homestead. As I was "the new boy on the block," I was honored to be chosen to cater the event from a list of about eight other approved caterers who were allowed to cater at the historic Tripp House. An added bonus was having my new restaurant which housed a state of the art, fully equipped kitchen where I could prepare the food I needed.

The woman who sat on the board gave me a simple direction, "I don't care what you serve, as long as it is beef!" I had decided to serve a lovely plated dinner of beef tenderloin with Béarnaise, accompanied by some lovely roasted garlic mashed potatoes, and fresh, crisp-tender haricot vert. The ladies wanted something dramatic for dessert and I told them that I would do a flaming Bananas Foster tableside. I decided to give them a show as I had them eating out of my hands that evening. I assembled my ingredients with great care. I decided to put the 151 proof rum in a small carafe and I did the same with the banana liqueur and Meyer's rum. I instructed one of my waiters who was posted at the light switch of the main dining area to kill the lights just as I was about to set my copper bottomed sauté pan aflame with the 151 proof rum.

The lights went out before I was ready because either I gave the signal too early or the waiter was afraid he would miss the exact moment to do as he had been instructed. I couldn't tell which carafe was which. I grabbed the one closest to me thinking it was the banana liqueur and I began to pour it liberally over my bubbling butter, brown sugar and sliced bananas. Before I could get a spoon to the mixture as it sizzled in the pan, it took to flame. WHOOOSH!!! It was like the space shuttle had just been launched as the flames soared above the sauté pan and almost reached the ceiling. The ladies clapped and cheered in adulation. I was thinking that this was probably the most excitement any of them had had in quite a long time. I was enjoying the attention and with great panache and care so as not to lose an eyebrow or an eyelash, I began to carefully turn the bananas with a large spoon. Much to my surprise, the stirring was adding more oxygen to the mix: the flames were becoming more ferocious and uncontrollable. The guests continued to cheer with delighted enthusiasm. I decided to enjoy the excitement, and, so to speak, just let the flames burn, and "glow" in the moment.

The next thing I knew, I began to hear a series of loud alarms blaring throughout the house. The woman who was a member of the board stood up. She did not look pleased. She ran to the kitchen where the security box was housed and silenced the alarms. It looked as if all would be well as the flames started to lessen in the pan. Relieved that the fire was now becoming more controllable and that the ladies found the whole event quite titillating, I looked out the French windows of the dining room. One of my nervous waiters had just brought me a tray with glasses of ice cream on it. But before I could dish out the first bananas onto the ice cream, the entire room was bathed in red light. The signal was turned off too late and the security company had called the fire department. Seven fire trucks now wailed in the parking lot of *The Tripp House*. The mobile intensive care unit was right behind them as well as several ambulances. Before I could serve the first dish of dessert, a fireman came into the dining room in full regalia. With ax in hand, he asked me if everything was all right. "It's just Bananas Foster," I replied. "Would you like one?" I extended a champagne glass filled with my creation. He looked at me as if I was crazy and left the room to search the rest of the house.

I don't know how it happened but it was not long before a local gossip columnist got hold of the story. The story was published and I was called "Jo Jo the Epicurean" and that the event was more like "The Towering Inferno," or "Joe Verses the Volcano." Actually, the publicity turned out to be priceless.

The woman on the Tripp House Board who arranged the party asked me to take Bananas Foster off my menu for future events at the house. I assured her that I would be more careful the next time. In fact, much to my surprise, months later, I realized that the cart on which I had set up my tableside service had been placed directly under the heat and smoke sensor. Moving the cart to a different side of the dining room and, of course, adding less of the flammable alcohol was a simple solution for future parties.

NOW YOU SEE IT—-NOW YOU DON'T

Another event that I catered at The Tripp House was set up by a woman who wanted to sponsor an engagement party for her son and daughter-in-law to be. The historical house would provide an intimate setting for the 50 or so guests who were invited for what primarily was a cocktail party.

The mother chose some lovely hors d'oeuvres to be passed. She also requested some stations featuring Baked Brie in Puff Pastry and a cheese appetizer I had devised called Floating Goat Cheese Islands in Roasted Tomato Sauce.

The woman selected some fine cookies and mini pastries for dessert, and then insisted that I order her a cake. In my experience, when guests are offered cookies and pastries, they seem to pass on the cake.

In any event I ordered a half sheet cake which I knew would easily feed about 50 people a small, yet adequate piece of cake, considering all the other sweet things that were being offered that evening.

I had put the half sheet cake on the buffet which sat majestically under a grand mirror in the dining room of the house. On a fluff of white fabric under which I had placed some tiny white Christmas lights, the period piece of furniture highlighted the cake beautifully, but I was unhappy with the cake sitting straight forward.

I took a few plates and tilted the cake on a forty-five degree angle toward the front of the buffet. It looked really elegant.

When the woman who arranged the party came into the dining room to inspect the house right before the party, I was certain she would comment on the striking cake display. I had placed huge trays of cellophane wrapped cookies on each side of the cake and displayed several huge trays of petite pastries on an adjacent antique table.

"That cake is so small," she boldly announced.

"It will be adequate," I calmly stated. "Look at all the other desserts that are here." I thought if anyone ate just one of everything displayed they would slip into sugar shock!

The party was about to begin, and the woman left the dining room without saying another word.

The hors d'oeuvres were well received as were a few other stations she had ordered featuring pasta and some carved meats with which cocktail sandwiches were made. In all, the event was going smoothly and waiters were reporting receiving many compliments throughout the evening.

A few hours into the event I decided it was time to cut the cake and make the desserts available to the guests. We readied a self-serve coffee station to accompany the sweet treats.

"Would you like to take a picture of the cake?" I asked the hostess. Most people like to take pictures before I begin to cut and serve the cake. Others like to say something like a "thank you" for coming or some "well wishes" for the guests of honor.

"No," was her curt reply. She just doesn't like the cake, I thought. I knew it would all change once she tasted a piece. I used one of the best, if not the best baker, in town. I never had anyone who didn't like this baker's cakes.

I began to cut the cake and with the assistance of a few waiters, we put the cut cake on lovely china plates. We put the plates on the dining room table so the guests could help themselves to the cake along with the cookies and various pastries on display.

And then it happened! I had about 25-30 pieces cut and on the table. The woman was frantically going in and out of the dining room, bringing plates of cake to guests. I was irritated because I had waiters to do that. The guests were invited to help themselves but not everyone ate the cake because there were so many other offerings.

Just as I was about to say something to the hostess, she exited the dining room. I was about to cut another row of cake pieces from the half sheet, when I saw the cake and then I didn't! It was like the sinking of the Titanic. As I had been cutting from the bottom edge of the cake and working my way upward, the cake had become top-heavy. Gently balanced on the plates I had used to prop it up for display, the cake was suspended almost upside down for a moment and then, before my disbelieving eyes, just sunk into the void behind the antique buffet!

At that precise moment, the hostess immediately came back into the dining room. My waiters and I instinctively moved like soldiers to the front of the buffet and hid the missing cake from view.

"I need a slab of cake," she announced. "My neighbor wants to take some home."

"We'll take care of it," I said as calmly as I could. "The boys will bring it out to you."

She quickly retreated from the room. The boys looked at me in astonishment. "A slab of cake?" they repeated in unison.

"Go get me those nice take out containers," I said.

I carefully took a few similar sized pieces of cake that were on the dining room table and tried to "smoosh" them together into what looked like… well a "slab" of cake.

The boys returned with the container and we placed the slab inside it. "Quick, bring this to her before she comes in here again," I ordered. One waiter grabbed the container and did as instructed.

"Should we pull out the buffet and get the rest of the fallen cake?" another waiter asked.

"No, I shouted. Then I caught myself and said in a softer voice, "We'll have to leave it behind there until the end of the party."

Luckily for me my hunch was correct. Few guests took cake and there were still about a dozen pieces sitting on the table when the hostess returned to the dining room a few minutes later.

"See," I said to her. "I told you there would be plenty of cake!" Little did she know just how much "plenty" there was.

TAKE IT OFF: EPISODE TWO

One June afternoon I got a call from a woman who informed me that she wanted to have an "Island Theme" party in the backyard of her home. I loved doing these kinds of parties. I booked the date and set up an appointment with the woman for later in the month when I would go to her home to check out the house and the garden where we would set up the party. The event was to be held in early August, so I had plenty of time to arrange for tent rental, chairs and tables and whatever else might have to be specially ordered for this particular outdoor party.

When I met with the hostess, she explained to me that she wanted the event to be as festive as possible. We planned a menu featuring a Caribbean Pulled Pork, so much better, in my opinion, than a whole roasted pig. I had done a similar party a few years before and ordered a roasted pig from a man who cooked pigs out in the country. The meat was tender, succulent and delicious, but it seemed to me that there was much less meat and more skin and bones. A whole roasted pig made a great display but I felt the pulled pork would be the way to go for this party. The pork would be served with fresh Keyser rolls and a selection of sauces for the pork. I had a sweet and sour sauce with pineapple, and a smoky barbeque as well.

We did a fried rice dish. A Caribbean red beans and rice was also on the menu in addition to a stir fry station that included fresh vegetables, shrimp, chicken, and a variety of sauces from which people could choose. It was a varied menu and included the cuisines of the South Pacific, Caribbean and a bit of Polynesian. The hostess was very excited.

I suggested that at the end of the evening we set up a flaming dessert station. We would toss pineapple, bananas and, of course, 151 proof rum, along with some other island liquors. I would set the mixtures ablaze in huge woks as the DJ played "Hot, Hot, Hot." We would then spoon the flaming concoction onto ice cream (in large bowls) which would be put on round trays that the waiters would carry on their heads as they danced through the crowd. It was going to be quite a show!

I also decided to bring some grass skirts along just for fun. I wasn't sure who, or when we would wear the skirts, but I brought them along with various island hats and flower leis.

The day of the party arrived. I had ordered huge palm leaves, various tropical flowers, and some huge bamboo sticks. I also had rented a huge fountain in which I would provide a fresh mojito mix and to which the hostess would add her own rum. We packed up the food and all the island props and decorations, and headed out to the site to set up the party.

The rental company did a great job with the tents. We began to set up the catering tables. When I looked at the grass skirts an idea came to mind. Instead of skirting the food tables with the fabric skirts I usually used, I decided to see if the grass skirts would work. As it turned out, the grass skirts were the perfect length for the long tables. I had a few dozen of them that I once had bought in bulk. We had enough skirts to drape all of the food stations and still had one or two skirts left over. I tossed the extra skirts under one of the food tables that I planned to use for the dessert.

The evening went without a hitch. The food was a big hit. I came out into the tent a few times throughout the service when I could steal away from the stir fry station to be sure everyone was having a good time.

An elderly lady pulled me aside and asked if I would dance with her later in the evening. She was old enough to be my grandmother, but I thought she was sweet and it wouldn't do any harm to dance with her. I told her that after we served the dessert, we were all going to dance, so that might be the perfect time for her to join us. She was delighted and I couldn't tell if she was very happy or just a bit intoxicated.

Finally, the time for the dessert show arrived. We moved the dessert table to the outskirts of the tents in full view of the guests. We set the huge woks on butane burners and began to sauté the fruits. The DJ cranked up the music. "Olé, olé, olé, olé, olé..." We were on our way!

I poured the rum from the bottles like Captain Hook. The flames towered high above the woks. No need to worry about fire alarms here! We were in the great outdoors. I began to spoon the raging inferno mix onto the large bowls of ice cream. Most stayed lighted long enough, as the waiters hoisted the trays above their heads and began to dance. They paraded throughout the crowd; I kept dancing behind the table that I had set up and kept the woks aflame as I continued to spoon the mixture onto the bowls of ice cream. We were generating plenty of excitement.

As we continued, one of my waiters came back to where I was working and began to do a series of great dance moves. He was studying to be a performer and was very talented. I usually hired waiters with these kinds of talents because we usually did something theatrical at our events. Also, many people with different talents often stop in to inquire because they are intrigued by the message on the window of the restaurant: *Where eating is a theatrical event!*

In any case, my dancing waiter was in full tilt. He began to jump and do leg splits. After a great display of energy and fancy moves, the expression on his face abruptly changed. I could see by the look that something was wrong. He either had pulled a muscle or who knows what else! He sort of danced towards me and turned his back to me. He had a gaping hole in his pants. He had split them from waist almost to... well let's just say his pants were really ripped.

As I had the grass skirts under the table, I threw one to him. He put the skirt on and continued to dance.

Our little, old, happy, (not quite sure if she was drunk) lady stood up and began to shout, "Take off the skirt; take it off!" She continued to shout, "Take it all off! Take off your pants!" She came over to me and began to dance. I had more control over the raging woks in front of me than I had over this situation.

She was in my face. I was trying to explain that I couldn't dance as I had to tend to the flames and the dessert. She pulled me away from the table and toward the dance floor area of the tent. Another one of my waiters took over at the dessert table as it was clear that I wasn't going to be able to get away from her.

I danced a bit to make her happy. The dancing at least stopped her from shouting. She seemed quite happy and content as we danced. Thank heavens! The song was soon over. I took one of the island flowers from my lei and presented it to her at the conclusion of the song. I gave her a hug and ran back towards the kitchen. A young man, who seemed a bit embarrassed by the episode, thanked me for being so nice to his grandmother. "No problem," I said, and continued to the sanctuary of the kitchen.

As the evening ended and we continued to pack up for the night, one of my waiters came to me and said that my dancing grandma wanted to say goodnight. I went out to the tent to wish her a good night. She seemed quite calm now and very sweet. "I had so much fun!" she exclaimed. "Thank you for dancing with me."

"My pleasure," I responded. "Now you behave yourself. And by the way, who's taking you home?"

"My grandson," she responded. The young man looked to be in is twenty's. I winked at him and told him to make sure he got her right home. He laughed and said, "We're going right home; I'm exhausted!"

I could tell by the look on her face and the gleam in her eye that, unlike her young grandson, she was still raring to go.

STAR STRUCK

I must admit that my affection for the theatre had remained strong over the years, and I had nothing but admiration for those who had the tenacity to succeed in the business. I was well aware that our local cultural center was planning to bring in a production of the off-Broadway comedy hit *Nunsense*. The production was the 20th anniversary all star tour. *Nunsense* was the second longest running musical in off-Broadway history. It won four Outer Critics Circle Awards including Best Off-Broadway Musical. The upcoming production starring Kaye Ballard, Georgia Engel, Mimi Hines, Darlene Love and Lee Meriwether was going to be in town for a few days and I wondered if I might offer the opportunity to cook for the cast and invite them to dinner. I thought maybe I could ask the producer if the stars would enjoy a night away from the clamor and attention of eating out publicly and come to my house for dinner.

I was not unknown to the promoters of the shows that came to town. On many occasions I had fed the companies of the shows that came to the theatre in our area. Most times those meals were served between the afternoon and evening shows. At other times, special parties would be given in a special performer's honor after the show. Those after theatre receptions allowed board members as well as financial backers to meet and greet the various personalities that came to town. I was very fortunate during those years to be the featured caterer.

Many people will remember, and I'm admitting my age to say I do, the late 60's television comedy, "The Mothers-in-Law," which starred Kaye Ballard. Among other various stage and television credits, Ms. Ballard is considered to be a comedic legend. Georgia Engel starred in Broadway's "The Boys from Syracuse," television's "The Mary Tyler Moore Show" and "Everybody Loves Raymond." Mimi Hines was married to the late Phil Ford and was Broadway's leading lady in "Funny Girl." She also appeared in TV's "Frasier." Darlene Love is the number one recording artist from Broadway's "Leader of the Pack" and a Rock and Roll Hall of Fame inductee. Lee Meriwether is a former Miss America who starred in TV's "Barnaby Jones."

It was quite a lineup of talent assembled in one place, and I wanted to cook dinner for them.

Several months before the production came to town, I called the touring company that was in charge of producing the show. They were not very hopeful about my offer. The show was on a tight schedule and meals most probably would be catered at the hotel where the cast was staying.

When the cast finally did come to town, Tony Nicosia, Jr., the executive director of the Broadway Theatre of Northeastern Pennsylvania, invited me to have lunch with the cast. Tony and I have been friends since childhood. He knew about my ill fated dinner and hoped lunch might be the next best thing.

I was appreciative of the invitation, but I really wanted to cook for the women. I did not want to go to a restaurant for dinner with them. I accepted the invitation hoping that I might be able to speak with the women myself and invite them to dinner.

We ate at a local restaurant that really wasn't busy that afternoon. As a result, most people didn't even notice that four stars were sitting in the restaurant. It seemed as if time had taken its toll on the life of "celebrity." We sat at a corner table that was somewhat secluded. I waited for the proper moment and then I popped the question, "How would you girls like to come for dinner one night during the run of the show?" All were gracious; Kaye Ballard was most enthusiastic. She informed me that their time was not their own and that such an event would have to be scheduled into their stay in the city. "What's your favorite food?" I boldly inquired.

Without a moment's hesitation, Kaye replied, "Eggplant!"

I was confident that I had planted the seed, and that my dinner would come to fruition. Kaye Ballard (whose real name is Catherine Gloria Balotta) was "not Italian for nothing." I knew she would just love my eggplant. An affirmative response to my invitation was a certainty. It was just a matter of time.

The show was to close on Sunday and I was contemplating whether I would go to see it again as I had already gone to the show on the Friday evening of the run. On Sunday afternoon, I received a telephone call from a gentleman who informed me that he was the company manager of *Nunsense*, the show that was playing at the cultural center. He said, "I'm calling to see if your invitation is still open for the cast to come to dinner."

I was delighted. "Of course! Tell me. When will they come?"

"Tomorrow night if that works for you," he said. He went on to inform me that the show would close that evening and, according to the stars' contracts, they needed a day off before traveling. As they would be staying in town until Tuesday morning, the schedule was clear for dinner on Monday evening.

Monday evening! I had less than 18 hours to put a dinner together for four legendary performers. I knew for sure that Kaye Ballard was expecting *eggplant*. I figured the menu was the least of my problems. Now I had to convince my wife that we were having company for dinner. "The dining room needs to be painted!" she exclaimed. "We can't have them here." The dining room looked fine to me, but Mary Ann was adamant about not having the celebrities come to our home.

The company manager was back in touch to set up a time. "Will 6 p.m. work for you?"

I said, "Sure, can you call me early tomorrow? Then I'll give you directions to the house and tighten up any other details you may need?" He agreed and hung up the phone. He had a time. I needed a place.

My dear friend Margaret was the only person I could think of who might come to the rescue.

"You want to do what?" she asked when I telephoned her.

"Just use your house," was my straightforward request. "It has to be low key." I added, "No one around, no posing for pictures or autographs." Margaret had four children and a husband. To this day, I don't know where she put the kids. She and her husband John agreed to stay at home and help me serve the dinner. I wanted as few people there as possible. She agreed.

I ran out to the supermarket and began to shop and plan the menu in one step. As eggplant was one of my featured dishes, I decided to prepare a Caprese salad of fried eggplant slices, with fresh tomatoes, fresh mozzarella and fresh basil. A balsamic reduction would round out the dish as a drizzle and garnish.

I made some homemade pasta with a tasty Bolognese sauce and I thought a simple Italian roast chicken might be a pleasant change from the "on the road" type dishes the women may have eaten during their tour. "I'll keep it simple and homey," I thought as I scurried through the market gathering my ingredients.

I prepared the eggplant, sauce and pasta at home in my kitchen. The plan was to transport these items on Monday afternoon to Margaret's house. The roast chicken I would assemble and bake at Margaret's, and my friend Tony said he would provide the wine.

Monday afternoon arrived quickly, but I was ready. When I arrived at Margaret's, she had the table beautifully set with lovely glass dinnerware. "Where did you get these?" I asked.

"I got them a long time ago on a sale and I never used them. I thought tonight would be a perfect time."

I got into the kitchen and began the tasks at hand. Margaret and her husband John worked alongside me and we had the dinner under control. The roast chicken was in the oven. The pasta water was on a slow simmer waiting for the homemade fettuccine. The eggplant Caprese was assembled on a beautiful platter and in the refrigerator; the Bolognese was slowly bubbling on a back burner of the stove.

"Now, no one knows about this?" I asked Margaret as I salted the waiting pasta water simmering slowly on the burner in front of me.

"No," she responded hesitantly. Her husband eyed her and I knew there was something to it.

"I promised them a quiet 'at home' dinner," I continued. "Please tell me it's going to be quiet."

"Oh, it will be," she responded. Her husband left the kitchen to put some flowers he had been arranging on the dining room table. I knew something was up.

It was 5:50 p.m. when the doorbell rang. Tony entered the room carrying several bottles of wine. "What did you get?" I asked anxiously while trying to pull the bottles away from him. The selections were fine. He had purchased a Chianti which I was sure Kaye would love, and he also had some California chardonnay as well as a sparkling champagne for a toast.

Tony sensed my concern. "Don't worry; I'll do the toast."

Thank goodness! He knew how I hated last minute surprises. It was enough that I pulled this off in little more than half a day, let alone come up with a toast at the last minute.

The doorbell rang promptly at six. "They're here!" I announced. I decided that as it was Margaret's house, she and her husband John should greet our guests at the door. Of course, I was not far behind.

THE ACCIDENTAL CHEF

Pleasantries were exchanged as the casually dressed women entered the house. "Where's Mimi?" I inquired. I asked the question as if I had known the star for years.

Kaye Ballard had the answer. "She's not feeling well."

"I'll send her a doggie bag," I said. Kaye thanked me and we hugged and kissed each other as well as the rest of our guests as we bid them enter the dining room and be seated for dinner.

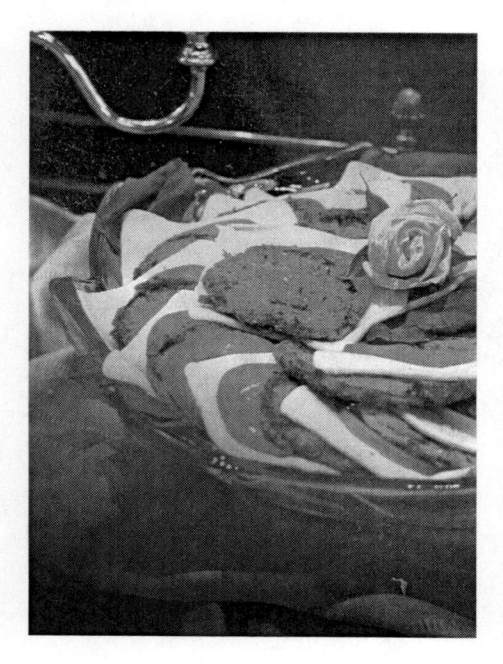

I quickly entered the kitchen to retrieve the eggplant Caprese. It would be a nice appetizer. Tony opened the Chianti and the festivities began.

The dinner unfolded just as planned. Just as I was about to have Margaret's husband carry out the platter of fettuccine, I abruptly ordered him, "STOP!"

"What's wrong?" he asked, startled by my sudden command. I grabbed a handful of chopped parsley and with great flourish threw it over the steaming pasta. Half of the parsley ended up on the kitchen wall. John still to this day taunts me that every now and then he finds parsley somewhere on the walls of his kitchen.

As the pasta was being served family style, the door bell rang. "I'll get it," Margaret insisted as she ran from the kitchen to the door. I could hear laughing and greetings being shared. It was Margaret's brother-in-law who "just happened to be in the neighborhood." After meeting everyone, he quickly left.

As the roast chicken made its exit from the oven, the doorbell rang again. This time I insisted on answering the door. It was the drama teacher of one of Margaret's children. "I didn't mean to interrupt," she said as she made her way right into the living room. The celebrities were very gracious and once they learned our visitor was a drama teacher, they were even more receptive. Of course, it was only a matter of time before they invited her to sit down for dinner.

The celebrities loved the food. Kaye asked if she could take some eggplant for the bus ride in the morning. They would be traveling to the next city where they were playing. I gave her a nice package along with some goodies for Mimi Hines.

The evening was very enjoyable and the stars were very gracious. I was so happy to have given them an opportunity to relax from the road and enjoy a home cooked meal even if it wasn't in my own home. Except for the two interruptions which the stars didn't seem to mind and which Margaret later admitted to having had arranged, no real damage was done. I kept my promise by asking to have not one photograph taken or any autograph requested from any one. Kaye Ballard did, however, send me a photo of herself and her four dogs the following Christmas.

I suppose the excitement of theatre and the people who make it happen will always have a warm spot in my heart. I know that night with the cast of *Nunsense* is one I'll always cherish.

THE BEEF THAT GOT AWAY

It was the second Christmas that "*Zuppa*!" was opened. We were very busy. In fact, that Christmas Eve, we did seven Christmas Eve dinners, two of which had to be delivered. Our customers were picking up the orders complete with instructions for warming them later in the evening.

I had done several beef tenderloins and had them individually wrapped in foil and labeled for each of the customers who had placed an order. I had separated the orders on a large steel work table that was in the center of the kitchen.

One lady had come in to pick up her dinner and I instructed two of my friends who were helping me with the holiday rush orders to carry the food out to her truck. She paid for her order and wished us all a happy holiday.

Later, a gentleman came into the restaurant and wanted to pick up his beef tenderloin for Christmas Eve dinner. I went into the kitchen. I could not find his beef on the steel table. I hurriedly checked the coolers both front and back, but I could not locate the meat. I was frantic. Finally, it occurred to me that as I had put the orders ready for pick-up very close together on the steel table, there was a possibility that the help had inadvertently put the second beef tenderloin into the truck of a woman who had an earlier pick-up. I thought, "Where else could that beef tenderloin have gone?"

I didn't know what to do. Where would I find another beef tenderloin at two o'clock on Christmas Eve afternoon? I went out to the front counter of the restaurant and calmly explained to the customer that I had planned to give him all of the food he had ordered for his Christmas Eve dinner, except for the beef tenderloin.

"Since this is the first time you've ordered from me," I explained, "I did not want to leave anything to chance. What time is your dinner?" I asked.

"Five o'clock," was his reply.

"Well, sir, I will bring you your Christmas Eve beef cooked, carved and garnished on a platter by a quarter to five."

"You will?" He was astonished, and equally delighted. "Yes, I will," I assured him. He paid for the rest of his order, and I helped him put everything into his car. When I returned to the restaurant, it was about 2:15 p.m. I had about two and a half hours to find his beef, finish cooking it, as it was par-cooked, slice it, garnish it and get it to his house. I felt like Santa Claus, but without countless elves. I was feeling a whole lot of pressure!

I frantically searched for the telephone number of the woman who had been in for the earlier order. I did not have it. All I had was her name. I looked her up in the telephone book, and luckily, her number was listed. I called her house and a very young voice answered which, I learned, belonged to the babysitter. I told her I was looking for the lady of the house.

"She's getting a pedicure," the young girl explained.

"What salon?" I asked.

"Not sure," was the reply.

"Do you have her cell phone number?" I pressed.

"Oh yes, I do." She had to retrieve the number from a desk drawer, but returned to the phone in a few minutes. I quickly jotted down the number and called the woman who I was hoping had the missing beef.

"Oh," she began to laugh. "I went home and put everything in the refrigerator. I wondered why you had given me two tenderloins!"

"Thank God she refrigerated it," I thought. She gave me her address and told me that when I got to the house I should just tell the baby sitter that I had her permission to get the beef from the refrigerator. It was almost 3 o'clock and I was frantic. Luckily for me, the house was only about fifteen minutes away. I instructed my sous chef Bruce to get the convection oven wickedly hot and to sharpen the carving knife.

Once I got back to the kitchen with the beef in hand, I put it in the hot oven and waited for the meat to cook. By then, it was about 4:15 p.m., but the meat was indeed cooked to the perfect temperature. I had just enough time to let it rest for ten minutes, carve it and get it on the platter. I wrapped the platter tightly in plastic wrap without a crease. It looked amazing! I grabbed a clean, white chef coat, grabbed the platter, got it and myself into the car and sped off to the home of my first time customer.

It was 4:50 p.m. exactly, when I arrived. "Here we are," I announced as I entered the house filled with family just about to sit at the dining room table beautifully set with china, crystal and lighted candles. I took the wrappings off the platter and proudly placed the beef on the table next to the other delights I had cooked, and the lady of the house had quite skillfully plated. Everyone complimented the beef and was truly amazed at the service I had delivered on Christmas Eve. I must admit, I myself was also truly amazed.

I thanked everyone and quickly bid them goodbye. I still had to get back to the kitchen and get one more order together for delivery before I went home to my wife who was anxiously awaiting my arrival since we had dinner reservations at a local restaurant for 7:30 p.m. I was looking forward to enjoying a meal that someone else was busy preparing.

THE BABY—-OUT WITH THE BATH WATER

A customer once asked me how to make chicken soup. "Your chicken soup is so delicious! Can you tell me what you do?" I painstakingly went through the entire process for making my chicken soup.

In order for the chicken meat not to be stringy, you remove the whole chickens from the simmering pot one hour after the initial cooking. Allowing the meat to cool and removing it from the bones, you ensure succulent meat for the soup. You then return the bones to the pot to continue cooking to make a rich stock for the soup. If you are unsure of the process, don't worry, the recipe can be found in the Recipe Section.

When that same inquiring client returned several days later, she expressed her disappointment in the technique I had given her in order to make a delicious chicken soup. "It just didn't taste like yours," she grumbled.

"Did you do what I told you?" I asked. "Yes," she responded. "I put the two whole chickens in the pot along with the bones, backs and necks, just like you told me. I even bought a new stock pot made of stainless steel, just like you said."

"So far, so good," I was listening intently.

"Then once it came to the boil, I put the heat on low and I began to skim off all the scum and residue that came to the top of the pot, just like you told me."

"Ok," I validated her following my specific directions.

"Then, she continued, "I kept skimming and skimming. When I could skim no more of the scum, I dumped all that dirty water and put fresh water in the pot."

After my jaw dropped to my knees and words could barely form in my mouth, I carefully formulated a sentence. "The dirty water?" I was aghast.

"Yes, with all that scum floating and such, I thought it best to throw out that first batch of water and start again."

"Love," I gingerly interrupted, "you threw out the soup!"

"I did?"

"Yes, that initial boil and skimming process had extracted the first elements of flavor for the soup," I was trying to be very clear.

"Oh," she answered, "I thought it would taste better without the dirty water!"

From that moment on, I always made sure someone who asked for a recipe either wrote it down or I wrote it down for them.

IT'S ALIVE!

One warm, summer Wednesday afternoon, a woman phoned me to inform me that her son who had just graduated from high school decided that he did not want a graduation party. Instead of a party he had requested a live lobster dinner at his home. His mother allowed the boy to invite two of his best friends and the rest of the guests would be family members. The party was planned for Saturday night, just two and half days away. When the woman told me who she was, I was aware that her father-in-law was a renowned architect in the area, probably retired now, but nevertheless, well traveled and well known.

"How many guests in all?" I inquired.

"Twelve," she replied.

"OK. Then suppose I round out the meal with some locally grown lime buttered corn on the cob, and sea salt encrusted baked potatoes," I suggested.

"Lovely, she replied, "and my father-in-law just loves coleslaw. Can you include that?"

"Of course, I can. Anything else?"

There was. "Maybe some cold shrimp as an appetizer, and I will supply my own cake."

"I don't think there will be any problem," I assured her. "I have to call my fishmonger and see if I can get the lobsters. How big do you want them?"

"At least two pounds each!" The order was done.

Immediately following the phone call, I called the seafood shop I had been dealing with and inquired if I would be able to have twelve 2 pound lobsters by Friday. The request was very short notice. It was Wednesday and I had to move quickly. Suddenly a rush of panic moved throughout my body. I couldn't remember the last time I had cooked a live lobster!

I remembered my days as a bus boy at *Billy's*, where the chefs used to taunt me with the live crustaceans. They would come at me with live lobsters in hand, their claws unencumbered. I thought they were ugly. Then they would tell me stories of how they would tickle the lobsters' bellies to put them to sleep and then put them in the cooler. One chef in particular would tell me to block my ears as he was about to plunge the live lobster head first into a pot of boiling water. "They scream like hell!" he would boast. I never witnessed the "drop." As a young man of about sixteen, I was too squeamish. I would always run out of the kitchen before the "lobstercide" took place.

I do remember that at the *Culinary Institute of America* where I had taken several extensive classes, a chef had done a demonstration by taking the tip of a sharp knife, and piercing the back of a live lobster's head. Too messy I thought!

I needed some help because I had very little time and very little experience with the dish I had to make in less than sixty hours. I e-mailed one of the chefs at the *CIA* who I had kept in contact with over the years since I studied there. I knew if anyone could help me, he could.

I asked the chef what he believed to be the best method. I expected some long and detailed explanation as to the preparation and procedure. I was aware of how the *CIA* was always very exact in every cooking method.

The e-mail was straightforward: Plunge the live lobsters head first into the boiling water and slap on the lid. Time them for about 16 minutes if each one is two pounds. Good luck, Chef.

That seemed too easy for me. I wondered if I added some white wine to the water, maybe some cut up lemon slices, a few bay leaves. Before I knew it, I was putting my own touch on Chef's recipe, but at least I had the basic cooking procedure.

I began to imagine crowding three or four pots on my client's stove in order to do the cooking. I really didn't like to clutter up people's homes too much especially if the dining room was an open space next to the kitchen. Since I didn't have time to visit the house before the party, I was not really set on cooking the live lobsters in the kitchen.

"Turkey fryers!" I thought. I had two turkey fryers in my garage. I had used them for a lobster boil I had done a few summers before. I cooked lobster tails along with clams, shrimp, red skinned potatoes, kielbasa, and corn for that party. I knew that those fryers were somewhere in my garage. I could purchase an additional one. With three turkey fryers, I could easily cook four lobsters in each one.

I decided to set up the whole makeshift kitchen in the garage. I could do the corn first, and then add the lobster boil seasonings to cook the lobsters. I could cook the baked potatoes in the kitchen oven. I had my plan.

I went to the fishmonger early on Friday morning. I brought two coolers with me, and he carefully placed some seaweed and wet newspapers in the coolers along with the lobsters. The coolers worked out fine with six of the meaty lobsters in each case. "These will keep for hours," the fishmonger instructed. I was glad to see that the claws of each lobster were fastened with thick rubber bands. "You remove those bands after you cook them," he added. I did know that. I had to write to the *CIA* for cooking instructions, but I knew you took the bands off after the lobsters were cooked and dead!

It was only when I was a teenaged busboy that those crazy chefs took off the rubber bands from the snapping claws while the lobsters were still alive so they could taunt me. I wished they could see me now.

I arrived at my client's home two hours before the event. The hostess had everything ready. Her table was lovely and she showed me huge platters she wanted each person to be served. Each one looked as though it could hold a 12 pound turkey. As I picked one up, it was almost a natural instinct for me to turn it around. "Hand painted in Italy" was printed on the back of the colorful platter.

"We got those in Positano, Italy," she proudly announced. "I have always wanted to use them."

I would have loved to have one; she had 12. "They are lovely," I said. "They will easily accommodate the lobster, baked potato and corn," I added. She showed me some smaller matching bowls that would be perfect for the coleslaw. I had brought some small ramekin-like containers for the drawn butter.

It was time to get to work. I got into the garage and set up the fryers. One of my waiters helped me fill them with water. As soon as we hooked up the propane tanks, we were on our way.

Minutes later the water began to tumble and boil. I decided to parboil the corn and then I would keep it covered and warm in a very low oven. As the hostess' kitchen had two huge *working* ovens, I was able to bake the sea salt encrusted potatoes in one and keep the second oven as a proofing oven to keep things warm.

When the potatoes were ready and the corn was placed in the holding oven, I knew it would only be about 16 minutes before dinner could be served.

Standing and chatting in a family room bar directly across from the open walled kitchen, the guests were enjoying the cold shrimp platter I had assembled. "Dinner will soon be served if you are ready," I informed the hostess. She graciously directed all the guests to take their places at the dining room table which was just a few feet from the main island of the kitchen. "Good call on the turkey fryers in the garage," I thought. I just hate when all the magic is on display. If it's a cooking demonstration type party or a really small house, I make compromises, but most times I like to stay hidden from view and remain unobtrusive.

As the guests were chatting and moving very slowly, I ran into the garage, added my ingredients to the boiling pots, and with the aid of two waiters, our 12 fated friends resting in the coolers were about to meet their maker.

I had instructed the waiter, who now had one lobster in each hand, to wait for the signal and then do the plunge. "NOW!" I shouted. We dropped the lobsters in synchronization. We retrieved the next six live lobsters and repeated our moves.

I had a stop watch and set it for 14 minutes. "I thought it was 16," one waiter said.

"It's going to take at least two minutes to get the pot lid off and get them out. Be attentive," I instructed. "When they come out, they go on these trays." I had six trays that I knew could accommodate two lobsters each. "I'll split the tails when they come out, and I'll slightly crack the claws. Then you boys get them into the kitchen and on to the waiting plates," I said. One of my woman assistants would ready the plates with the corn and baked potato and a small drawn butter cup. The coleslaw sides would be served by other waiters on the coat tails of the ones serving the platters. "You got it?" I asked my crew. They all nodded in agreement, but I knew I would have to bark out the orders once more when the time came.

Fourteen minutes later, our plan was in action. The guests were seated by now. Drink in hand, the grandfather of the young graduate bid a toast.

When the meal was completed, the grandfather approached me. "I have eaten many live lobsters all over the world," he disclosed. "I must tell you, that was the best one I ever had!"

I *humbly* replied, "You have to know just how to cook them."

He then proceeded to tell me that the coleslaw was the best he had ever eaten. I was so flattered, I told him my secret. "I put sweetened condensed milk in it."

CELEBRATING THE PAST ON SEVERAL LEVELS

In the fall of 2009, my wife Mary Ann and I celebrated 25 years of marriage. To mark our anniversary, I planned a three week trip to Europe. We began with a two week Mediterranean cruise and afterwards enjoyed an additional week in Rome. We literally ate our way through seven countries, starting in Barcelona, Spain; then Nice, France; Florence, Italy; and Tolfa, Italy, where I cooked at a small bed and breakfast called Fontana del Papa. Then, it was on to Naples, Italy; Istanbul, Turkey; Athens and Mykonos, Greece; Split, Croatia; and finally Venice, Italy. We took a train from Venice to Rome and spent our last week there. There will be wonderful recipes from that adventure in the Recipe Section but now I would like to tell the story of our waiter at the Aldrovandi Palace in Rome. He provided us with quite a theatrical escapade, and also proof that all around the world it seems true that good help is hard to find.

ARRIVEDERCI PESCE! or GOODBYE FISH!

After our two week sojourn across the Mediterranean, Mary Ann and I spent a not-so-restful night in Venice. I had decided that we would stay at the same hotel we visited on our honeymoon. Without giving too much away, let it suffice to say that much had changed in twenty-five years, except for the hotel. The place had not changed a bit. There were the same rooms, the same beds, the same sheets.

As we arrived in Venice toward the end of October, the weather was cool. I'd say temperatures were in the low 60's. For the Venetians, this time of year was the onset of winter, so the heat had been turned on in the hotel. I spent a sleepless night tossing and turning in the terribly warm room. The sheets were starched with what I thought must have been Elmer's glue which made the bed very uncomfortable. I was looking forward to the morning when we would take a high speed train to Rome. At one point, when I could take the heat no more, I got out of bed and flung open all the shuttered windows in the room, without regard if cat, bat or mice would enter. By morning, the room finally cooled down to a bearable temperature.

We boarded the train the next morning, and four hours later, we found ourselves in Rome. We checked into our hotel, here again, the same one we had visited on our honeymoon. To our delight, this place had changed and was now considered a five star hotel. It had been a long day and we were tired. We decided to stay at the hotel which had many amenities, and after a restful nap, we were ready for dinner.

Rather than battle with the hustle and bustle of the city, we opted to stay at the hotel and have dinner in a small restaurant "grill" next to the lobby bar.

There, we met our waiter Simone. He was gallant. With much bowing, and pomp and circumstance, he began to describe the specials for the evening. Simone went on to tell us that he had worked at the Ritz in London and had served Queen Elizabeth several times.

I assured him, "We're just Mary Ann and Joseph. So relax. I have only one request. I would like to order our meal completely in Italian." Mary Ann looked horrified, but I knew I could handle the task at hand. I began with the antipasto which for us would be a simple Caprese Salad. We would also share a simple dish of pasta. For Mary Ann,

I ordered the pollo (chicken) and for me the pesce (fish.) The ambiance in the grill room was reminiscent of the thirties, very tailored and streamlined in design in hues of hunter green, rose and rich mahogany.

The piped-in music played: Parole, parole, parole (literal translation: words, words, words).

Ascoltami (Listen to me). I asked the assistant waiter Andrea as he passed by, "Andrea, ma che cosa significa 'parole?'"/But what is the meaning of parole? I was looking for a much deeper, richer meaning.

"Words!!" And that was all he said.

In the meantime, our pasta was served with great panache as Simone showered Parmesan cheese atop our dishes from a hand held grater, all the while announcing, "Buon appetito!"

As was all the pasta in Italy, this one was superb. Out of the corner of my eye, I saw the bar area outside the grill with its polished marbled floors. Much to my astonishment, at that precise moment, I saw Simone who slipped and fell flat on his rear end. I wondered how that maneuver had flown with the Queen. As he got up, he caught the look of astonishment on my face. I think he was rather embarrassed since he thought no one had noticed his tumble. A few minutes later, he came into the dining room and whispered to me, "Signor, did you see what happened to me out there?"

"Don't worry about it, Simone," I replied. "Just relax, and bring our dinners."

"Si, signor," he replied, and in a very few minutes he returned with Mary Ann's chicken dish, but he didn't have my dinner, a fresh sea bass.

I told Mary Ann to start to eat her dinner as mine was sure to be along momentarily. Much to my surprise, about fifteen minutes later, Simone returned and asked us if there would be anything else. "Simone, I asked quietly, "Dove il pesce? (Where is my fish?)"

"Oh, mamma mia," he groaned, slapping his hand against his forehead. "Oh, signor, mi dispiace!" (I am sorry!) Obviously, Simone, *waiter to the Queen of England*, had completely forgotten my dinner. He ran back to the kitchen, and returned, very composed and again very dramatic. "Signor, our chef will prepare for you a dish that is an only one of its kind in this region. It is a kind of pasta that is made only here in Lazio. It is called pacheri, and I know you will love it. Again, remember, it is only here in this region of Italy that you can have such a dish."

"Ok," I replied. Quite honestly, I just wanted my fish, but if this is how Simone wanted to make amends, who was I to argue?

About ten minutes later he returned with his "pacheri," a tubular pasta reminiscent of rigatoni, only wider and without ridges. It seemed to me as if the dish had some eggplant in it and a sauce, that when I tasted it, reminded me of canned tomato paste. It was so not good, but I didn't have the heart to tell Simone. I ate it, and later found out that only the pasta was on the house. That gesture made things simpler. Needless to say, I wouldn't have paid for my nonexistent/ poor substitute meal. We left the restaurant without further ado, and only once more returned for a rather expensive dinner. That evening, I had a great meal which featured a wonderful new soup. That recipe, Zuppa Di Vedure a la Roma can be found in the Recipe Section.

As for the pacheri, when I returned to America, I devised my own version of it. I hope you will try the recipe in the Recipe Section. If you can't find pacheri, use rigatoni or penne. It will be a wonderful meal.

DESSERT: THE ICING ON THE CAKE

RETURN TO "LA DOLCE VITA"

While our ship was docked in Civitavecchia for two days, I arranged to be taken to Fontana del Papa in Tolfa, about a ninety minute drive from the port. Quite a long time earlier, on line, quite by accident, (Is that redundant?) I had met a woman named Assuntina. It was about a year before my anniversary trip with Mary Ann.

During that time, I came to learn that Assuntina had earned her university degree in French Literature at Rome University, and had taught, as I had, for over 20 years. She also worked as a court translator. She had a passion for language and she very easily communicated with me for over a year via email. I told her that one of my dreams was that while I was in Italy, I wanted to have the opportunity to cook in a truly domestic setting. I did not want the commercialism of a cooking school like those in Bologna or some other big city. Assuntina went on in her communications with me to describe how in 2000 she had become the owner of Fontana del Papa, a ruined farmhouse with an olive grove that was suffering from years of complete abandonment in the small village of Tolfa. In her dreams, she saw a vision of how the property once shone—- the olive grove bearing rich fruit to process the best olive oil in the world. That oil she would share with her visitors and guests. There was a sense of tenacity, passion and love about this woman.

She went on to tell me about her cook Matilde who taught the cooking classes and how the recipes were not written down but were stored only in Matilde's head. This was what I had been looking for. I wanted to relive an experience much like those I had shared with my mother and my grandmother. I knew I had found such a place in Fontana del Papa as soon as I approached the house where I would meet Matilde.

As I walked up the cobblestone steps that led to Matilde's kitchen in the back of the villa, I saw a broom and a pail outside the door. I was home. Both my mother and my grandmother always kept a broom and pail outside the doors of their kitchens. I knew cleanliness was obviously a priority. These kitchens were temples, places that one revered since the work that took place in them was considered sacred.

That day, I entered the kitchen gingerly as it was obvious Matilde was already at work preparing her "mise en place" (everything in its place), getting ready for the day's lesson and afterwards, enjoying lunch. Rather pretty, with blond hair and blue eyes, she was a typically northern Italian, maybe sixty years of age. My grandmother and mother, of course, were Calabrese, with olive complexions and dark eyes. In a short time, I would soon discover that those qualities were the only differences in the three women.

A short "buon giorno" was exchanged; there would be time for conversation later. Right now Matilde was all business. She had a meat cleaver in her hand and was preparing the chicken drumsticks for our cooking which would take place later. With a mighty whack, the cleaver struck the bone of the chicken leg. Matilde had that power. Here was a woman who had the "stock" to be a cook. No formal training, just passion. I looked at her and saw my grandmother. I saw my mother. My grandmother and my mother both had that same kind of

Torta di mele

"stock." Cleavers, hammers, butcher knives, hand cranked meat grinders: these were their tools. Nothing squeamish about this kind of woman! Each was strong and dauntless in the task at hand, preparing the meal. Matilde was gracious, but very much at work. I was directed out of the kitchen and onto the terrace for some cappuccino and baked goods that she had made earlier that morning.

When it was time to begin cooking, Matilde had everything in its place. The flour and potatoes for the gnocchi were measured. The chicken legs and the fresh sage for the chicken cacciatore were ready for the skillful hands that would soon create magic.

As I stood in that kitchen awaiting Matilde's instruction, I was intoxicated with familiar smells: the pungency of fresh garlic, the verdant lemony scent of parsley and, of course, basil. I was truly home. I was in a remote village in Italy thousands of miles from where I had lived my entire life, but, there in that kitchen, everything seemed welcomingly familiar.

"Cominciamo." (We begin.) Matilde spoke as she handed me a paring knife to begin peeling the cooked potatoes. Matilde's English was broken but understandable. A translator was there just in case.

As she began, I was truly amazed— amazed at a woman of her resourcefulness. She was very strict in her kitchen, but in a loving way. She reminded me of my grandmother when she scolded me as I was about to put lemon in the pesto. "No, no limone!" she commanded. She did not want lemon in the pesto. I always put lemon in my pesto. I think it brightens the flavor and keeps the basil greener. But this was Matilda's kitchen and I was in Rome, (actually, north of Rome), but as always, it's good to remember the ever true cliché, "When in Rome, do as the Romans do."

As we made the gnocchi and floured the boards and tea towels on which we worked, Matilde would collect the excess flour and put it back in the flour bin.

She took the potato peelings, the vegetable scraps, even the egg shells. Some things were fed to the chickens, others to the pigs, and other refuse was used as compost. Both of my grandparents did that; I felt like I was young and, once again, at home in my grandmother's kitchen.

Matilde carefully gave me the approximate amounts of the ingredients for the recipes that we made. I wrote them down as we cooked in the modern kitchen of the refurbished farm house.

For me, that experience was amazing. I had come full circle. By that time, cooking had become my profession. I had come to a distant village north of Rome only to find that I had returned to what I had known for so many years. I had come to return to myself, to who I was, to where I came from, to what was really important, to what I did well. Standing in that place gave me great joy!

Because I so value what has happened to me, especially having the courage to embrace the real me, Joseph the Cook, I am eager to share so much with so many. I feel I needed to write this book, to express simple truths about who I am, and to share a wonderful realization.

I hope you try some or all of the recipes in this book. In my writing them, my cooking them and most of all in my eating them, I found these were dishes that took me back to people, places and events in my life that I fondly treasure in my heart and in my soul. For me it is a personal journey; for you, I hope a laugh, and at least a good meal.

Food has that ability to take us back. The tastes and smells can tangibly be experienced, but more importantly so can the love. I hope you experience that. Love is the one ingredient that is not listed in the recipes but is a very important component to each and every dish that is shared here. You can never put too much love into your cooking. When love is an ingredient, you feed not only the body but also the soul.

When I woke up that first day after losing my job, I felt sad, lonely and confused. Yet, I know that human beings are amazing machines. God created each of us with resilience. It's there. We have to look for it. When we are most alone and most vulnerable, we often turn outward for help. Looking to others is certainly a healthy step toward change and recovery, but unless we turn inward first, no one or anything outside can help us make a new beginning. Perhaps when we go inward, we meet God and his plan for us—the only plan that will make us truly happy because it is the plan that allows us with grace and freedom to become who we truly are.

One day, a friend of mine who had also lost his job later in his life came into my restaurant sad and depressed. He had found a job in sales but he reveled in the glory of his previous job where he felt he was king. "You sell chemicals; I make soup. For God's sake," I chided him. "If you don't give value to what you do, who will?" I went on to explain to my friend who was having a pity party that soon after I started making soup, someone said to me, "My father always said, if you're going to dig a ditch, dig the best ditch you can." Obviously, that person likes my soup, and he appreciates what I do and my attitude toward my new life's work.

As I turned to culinary as the start of a new career, that choice forced me to take an inward look. I came to answer some questions about myself. I turned to comfort, to those things that made me feel good, the things I knew best. The food I enjoyed growing up, my family and the love we shared making and eating those dishes: these were and remain the most familiar, the most gratifying and now, in this exciting adventure of dramatic change, the most constant.

I guess in that sense, as someone once said to me, I was lucky. Still, I prefer to think that I was so much more than lucky. I was blessed, no, doubly blessed. So many things in my life may seem to have been accidental. Yet, as I look back on my journey, and the joy it has given me, I know I have found my niche in what I prefer to call the Grand Design. My fondest hope for each of you is that the recipes you find in this book will bring you into a deeper bond with the people you love. May each meal bring you to a new awareness about the gift of *simple cooking*. Is there any better gift than that loving gesture which sustains us all as we nourish one another?

May each meal you prepare be blessings on you and those you serve.

RECIPE SECTION INDEX

Page

BREADS

69	Basic White Bread
70	Focaccia
71	French Bread
72	My Mother's Raisin Bread
73	My Mother's Zucchini Bread

ANTIPASTI

74	Clams Casino
75	Floating Islands of Goat Cheese in Roasted Tomato Sauce
76	French Bread Pizza with Bermuda Onion and Red Pepper Marmalade
77	Jazz
78	Leek and Goat Cheese Quiche
79	Polenta Squares with Spicy Bolognese

SALADS AND SLAWS

80	Caprese Nicoise
81	Eggplant Caprese
82	Greek Salad from Mykonos
82	Joseph's Cole Slaw
83	My Grandfather's Green Bean and Potato Salad
84	Red Cabbage and Mango Slaw

SOUPS

85	French Onion Soup
86	Italian Minestrone
87	Mrs. Williams' Meatball Stew
88	My Grandfather's Fusilli e Ceci
89	My Grandfather's Minestra
90	My Mother's Chicken Soup
91	Salmon Corn Chowder
93	White Pasta Fagiole
94	Zuppa Di Vedure a la Roma (Vegetable Soup)

VEGGIES

95	Escarole with White Beans
96	My Grandfather's Giambotta
97	My Grandmother's Fried Potatoes
97	My Grandmother's Spinach and Potatoes
98	My Mother's Stuffed Artichokes
99	My Mother's Stuffed Zucchini Boats

PASTA

100	Butternut Squash Ravioli with Brown Sage Butter
101	Gnocchi
102	My Grandmother's Manicotti
103	My Grandmother's Pasta
104	Pacheri Alle Melanzane

POLENTA/RICE

105 Coconut Rice
106 My Grandmother's Polenta
107 My Grandmother's Thursday Baked Rice
108 Rice, Dried Cherry, and Almond Dressing
109 Suppli al Telefono-Arancini-Rice Balls

SAUCES

110 Balsamic Glaze
110 Béarnaise Sauce
111 Joseph's Easy Spicy Bolognese
112 Matilde's Pesto
112 My Grandfather's Spaghetti Sauce
114 Roasted Tomato Sauce
114 Spicy Barbeque Sauce
115 Sweet and Sour Sauce

MEATS
BEEF/PORK/VEAL

116 Beef Braciole
117 Filet of Beef Tenderloin
118 Joseph's Oven Roasted Citrus Orange Glazed Pork Tenderloin
119 My Grandfather's Meatballs
120 My Grandfather's Veal Cutlets
121 My Mother's Swiss Steak
122 Pork Saltimbocca
123 Pulled Pork
124 Standing Rib Roast
125 Veal Oscar

POULTRY

126   My Mother's Fried Chicken
127   My Mother-in-Law's Sunday Chicken
128   Pollo Alla Cacciatore

SEAFOOD

129   Joseph's Asian Citrus Grilled Salmon
130   Joseph's Pan Seared Citrus Orange Grouper
131   Live Lobster
132   Scallops Sir Galahad
134   Shrimp Scampi The Best!
135   Trout Amandine
136   Wahu (Wahoo) and Potato Cakes with Red Cabbage and Mango Slaw

DESSERTS

138   Apple Torta
139   Bananas Foster
139   Mary Ann's Chocolate Pepper Cookies
140   My Grandmother's White Cookies from Calabria
141   Pistachio Cake
142   Yum Yum Cake

A KISS FROM ABOVE

143   A Kiss From Above
144   My Date and Nut Bars, One of Joseph's Favorites

BREADS

Basic White Bread

I remember eating thick slices of this warm bread with melted butter or sometimes with the melted butter and a light sprinkling of sugar!

Makes 2 loaves

5 to 6 cups of all-purpose flour

2 packages of active dry yeast

2 cups of whole milk

⅓ cup of sugar

⅓ cup of vegetable shortening

2 teaspoons salt

2 eggs

In a large bowl combine 2½ cups of flour and yeast. In a small saucepan, heat milk, sugar, shortening and salt until warm (NOT HOT). Stir the mixture until the shortening has melted.

Add the lukewarm liquid mixture to the dry mixture in the bowl. Now add the eggs and beat with electric mixer at low speed for about a minute as you scrape down the sides of the bowl. Now beat an additional three minutes at high speed. After mixing, using your hands, stir in the remaining flour minus ½ cup to be used for kneading later.

The dough will become stiff, sticky and very firm. Turn out the dough on a lightly floured board or marble slab. Using the heels of your hands, knead in the rest of the flour until the dough becomes smooth and elastic. This will take about eight minutes. Place the kneaded dough in a lightly greased large bowl. You can use some vegetable shortening to grease the bowl. Turn the dough around once or twice to ensure that all the surfaces of the mass are lightly greased. Cover the bowl with a tea towel and let rest in a warm place until the dough has doubled in size- about 2 hours. When risen, punch the dough down and divide into two equal pieces. Cover again and let the dough rest about 15 minutes. Shape the two pieces into loaves and place in lightly greased (use vegetable shortening) 8 x 4 x 2 inch loaf pans. Cover the pans with tea towels and let rise again until nearly double in size- about one hour.

Bake in a pre-heated 375° oven for 35-40 minute. My grandmother always removed the breads from the pans and tapped the bottom. If the loaf sounds hollow, it is done. She would then tip the loaves slightly upside down in the pans to cool for a few minutes before putting them on a wire rack to cool.

Focaccia

This is a versatile bread that can be eaten with soups, stews or any other comfort food! You can put thin sliced tomato and onion over the top before you slip it into the oven to bake.

Makes 1 large Focaccia

2 packages active dry yeast

2 cups of warm water

1 tablespoon of sugar

5 cups of unbleached flour plus 2 tablespoons and a bit more for working the dough

1½ teaspoons of Kosher salt

½ cup of extra virgin olive oil

1 teaspoon of chopped fresh rosemary

1 tablespoon grey salt and 1 teaspoon black pepper

In a small bowl combine the yeast, warm water, sugar and 2 tablespoons of flour and stir until incorporated. Let the mixture rest for about 15minutes. It will become frothy.

Meanwhile in a large bowl, combine 5 cups of flour and 1½ teaspoons of salt. Make a well in the center of the flour. Pour the foamy yeast mixture into the center of the well and add about 2 tablespoons of olive oil. Begin to work with your hands around the wall of the flour incorporating it into the liquid. Continue until all of the flour and the liquid yeast mixture is combined and begins to make dough.

Sprinkle some more flour (a few tablespoons) on a work surface and knead the dough with the heels of your hands for about 10-12 minutes. The dough will become very smooth and elastic- like. If the dough is sticky or your hands are sticky, just sprinkle a bit more flour to help keep the dough moving on the work surface.

Shape the dough into a ball and place it in the large bowl coating the entire mass with a tablespoon of olive oil. Cover the bowl with a damp tea towel or some loose plastic wrap and put the bowl in a warm place to rise. The dough should double in size. This will take about 40-45 minutes. When the dough has risen, punch it down and let it rise again for another half hour.

Take another tablespoon of olive oil and spread on a cookie sheet about 11 x 15 inches. Put a few more tablespoons of flour on your work surface and spread and work the dough into a rectangle approximately the same size as the sheet pan. Place the formed dough on the greased cookie sheet and work the dough to fit the pan. Cover the pan with plastic wrap or tea towel and let rise another 20 minutes. When the dough has risen for the final time in the pan, use your fingers to dimple the dough into a uniform pattern. The dimple marks should be in straight rows over the entire surface of the dough.

Sprinkle the dough with the rosemary, 1 tablespoon of the grey salt and some freshly ground black pepper. Drizzle about ¼ cup of extra virgin olive oil over the entire surface of the dough.

Bake in a 425° oven for 18-20 minutes until golden.

French Bread

Because of the great love of bread I had from my childhood, I took a class in college called the Biology of Bread, Wine and Cheese. I loved the making of the bread, the cheese and, of course, the wine, but I hated the biology! Here is a simplified version of the bread we made. (You can use the bread for the crouton for the French Onion Soup) or toast slices for dipping in the Floating Islands of Herbed Goat Cheese. (See Recipe Section.)

Makes 4 loaves

Pinch of sugar

2½ cups of warm water —-about 110　F.

3 packages of active dry yeast

8 cups of all-purpose flour

4 teaspoons salt

Additional lukewarm water

¼ cup of cornmeal for sprinkling on baking sheets

In a large glass measuring cup or bowl, stir the sugar into the 2½ cups of warm water and sprinkle the yeast over the top. Let the mixture stand for 5 or 6 minutes until it has "bloomed" frothy. Place the flour and the salt in a large bowl and add the yeast mixture. Using your hands, combine the mixture to make dough. On a floured board surface, knead the dough 8-10 minutes until smooth and elastic. Sprinkle additional flour (this ensures that no crust will form on top). Cover with a towel and let rise at room temperature for about 3 hours. Sprinkle 2 large baking sheets with corn meal.

Punch down risen dough and knead for a minute. Then divide the dough into 4 equal pieces. Shape each piece into a long loaf and place on the prepared baking sheets- 2 loaves per sheet. Cover the dough with tea towels and let rest in a warm place for about 40 minutes. Pre-heat oven to 425°.

Slash the loaves diagonally several times with the edge of a very sharp knife. Either brush or spray (using a clean spray bottle) with additional warm water. Bake for 15 minutes then reduce the heat to 350° and bake an additional 15 - 20 minutes or until the loaves are golden brown.

My Mother's Raisin Bread

My mother made this bread every Easter, but it can be enjoyed anytime of the year!

Makes 1 large loaf

3 tablespoons of sugar

2 eggs

1 cup of warm whole milk

2 packages active dry yeast

4 cups of all purpose flour

1 teaspoon salt

6 tablespoons melted butter

1 cup dark raisins that have be coated with about ¼ cup of flour

In a glass bowl or measuring cup, stir the yeast and 1 teaspoon sugar with the warm milk. Let stand about 5 minutes until the mixture is frothy. Sift together the flour and salt in a large bowl. In a medium bowl, mix the remaining sugar, cooled melted butter and eggs. Stir the yeast mixture into this bowl. Pour the liquid mixture into the flour mixture and combine with a wooden spoon to make a soft dough. On a floured board, knead the dough for about 10 minutes until smooth. Place the dough in a large bowl that has been lightly oiled or buttered. Cover with a towel and let rise in a warm place until doubled in size about 45minutes. Grease a 12 x 4 inch loaf pan. Knead the raisins into the risen dough and shape into a loaf; place loaf in the prepared pan. Let stand in a warm place for 30 minutes. Place in a preheated 350° oven and bake 40 minutes or until loaf sounds hollow when the underside is tapped. Ice, if you like, when loaf is completely cooled.

Icing

½ pound of confectioners' sugar

1 tablespoon of lemon juice

1 teaspoon of good vanilla extract

Blend all ingredients together and ice the top of the loaf when completely cooled.

My Mother's Zucchini Bread

Here is yet another "great" something else Mom made with the countless zucchini that came from my grandfather's garden, a delicious bread that goes great with a smear of creamery butter!

Makes 2 large or 4 small loaves

3½ cups all-purpose flour

2 cups sugar

1 cup vegetable oil

3 eggs

1½ teaspoons baking soda

¾ teaspoon baking powder

1 teaspoon cinnamon

¾ teaspoon nutmeg

1 teaspoon salt

2 teaspoons vanilla (not imitation)

2 cups of grated zucchini

1 cup of chopped walnuts or pecans

1 cup of raisins

1 can (8 ounce) crushed pineapple, drained

Preheat oven to 350°. Cream the sugar, oil and eggs with an electric beater. Add combined baking powder, baking soda, salt, cinnamon, nutmeg, and flour. With a spoon, fold in grated zucchini, nuts and raisins, pineapple and vanilla. Blend gently. Pour into greased bread pans. Bake in a 350° oven for 50 minutes. Check with a toothpick to see if the toothpick comes out clean. Remove from pans and cool upright on a rack.

ANTIPASTI

Clams Casino

What I like about Billy's clams casino is that the clams are removed from their shells and a stuffing is made which is then put back into the shell and baked.

Serves 6

24 clams shucked (reserve juice)

8 slices of bacon

1 small onion chopped fine

1 red bell pepper diced small

Juice of one lemon

¼ cup dry vermouth

¼ cup of clam juice or liquor that comes from shucked clams

2 tablespoons chopped parsley

Salt and pepper to taste

¼ stick of butter cut into small dice

1 cup of seasoned breadcrumbs

Drizzle of olive oil

Chop up the "meat" of the shucked clams and set aside. Save juices in a small bowl.

Chop bacon into small pieces and then render in hot skillet. Remove bacon pieces with slotted spoon. Drain off some of the bacon grease from the skillet.

Add chopped onion and red pepper to bacon fat, return to medium heat and sauté gently until softened. Deglaze pan with lemon juice and vermouth and clam juice. Let reduce until almost dry. Take skillet off heat and add breadcrumbs and chopped clams.

Mix with wooden spoon until well combined and slightly cooled.

Add chopped parsley and season with salt and pepper to taste. Stuff each shell with clam mixture, sprinkle a bit of breadcrumbs on top, dot with a small piece of butter, and place in oiled shallow baking dish. Drizzle all the clams with some extra virgin olive oil and bake in 375° oven just till the bread crumbs are browned and the clams have cooked without becoming rubbery, about 15-20 minutes. Serve straightaway.

You can stuff the shells in advance. Refrigerate the shells and bake them later. You may have to increase cooking time if you transfer the clams directly from the refrigerator to the hot oven.

Floating Islands of Goat Cheese in Roasted Tomato Sauce

This is my version of a dish I had at Mon Ami Gabi in the Paris Hotel Las Vegas. Cut my crusty French bread (See Recipe Section) on a diagonal and toast for dipping!

Serves 4-6

8 ounces of fresh soft goat cheese

4 ounces of cream cheese at room temperature

1 tablespoon of honey

½ teaspoon of fresh thyme

1 tablespoon of fresh chopped parsley

1 clove of minced garlic

1 teaspoon of black pepper

2 teaspoons of Kosher salt

Combine all of the above in food processor and blend until smooth and creamy. Refrigerate for one hour.

Prepare Roasted Tomato Sauce (See Recipe Section). Ladle sauce into chafing dish. Using an ice cream scoop, put dollops of cheese mixture in the sauce. Sprinkle with chopped parsley. Serve with crostini, toasted bread or breadsticks for dipping.

French Bread Pizza with Bermuda Onion and Red Pepper Marmalade

Serves 6-8

This is an original appetizer that I devised sailing to Bermuda while I was making an appearance as a Guest Chef on Holland America's ms Veendam. The ship had no Bermuda onions and we substituted Spanish onions and were rewarded with the same delicious results.

1 loaf of crusty French bread cut in half lengthwise. You can make my French bread (See Recipe Section) or buy a favorite of your own.

Bermuda onion and Red Pepper Marmalade (Recipe follows)

2½ cups of Goat Cheese or grated mozzarella or Fontina cheese

¼ cup of good quality extra virgin olive oil

Finishing grey salt and freshly cracked pepper

Pre-heat oven to 350°. Brush olive oil on both halves of the French bread. Dopple the marmalade onto the bread halves. Sprinkle each half with half of the cheese. Bake until crisp and bubbly— about 15 minutes. Finish with a touch of grey salt and freshly cracked pepper.

Bermuda Onion and Red Pepper Marmalade

4 cups thinly sliced Bermuda onions

2 small red peppers, small dice

2 tablespoons canola oil

1 teaspoon salt

¼ teaspoon freshly ground black pepper

¼ cup sugar

¾ cup of white vinegar

Sauté the onion with salt and pepper in hot oil in a skillet over medium heat. Stir intermittently until the onions are very golden. Add the red peppers and cook for 1 minute. Add the sugar and cook for 2 minutes, stirring constantly. Add the vinegar and cook for 1 minute. Cover and let simmer for about 45 minutes. Cool before making pizza.

Jazz

A great appetizer served alongside carrot, celery sticks and fresh whole scallions, crackers and breadsticks

Serves 4- 6

The Cottage Cheese and Chives

1 (16 ounce) container of 4% milk fat cottage cheese

4 tablespoons of freshly chopped chives

1 teaspoon of Kosher salt

½ teaspoon of freshly grated pepper

Combine all ingredients in a bowl and let the mixture sit in the refrigerator for 2 hours.

Serve with bread sticks and crackers.

The White Bean Salad

1 (15 ounce) can of cannellini or great northern beans rinsed and drained

2 cloves of minced garlic

1 tablespoon of finely minced parsley

½ medium white onion diced small

½ cup of extra virgin olive oil

¼ cup of red wine vinegar

Salt and pepper to taste

Combine all of the ingredients in a bowl and let sit in the refrigerator for 2 hours.

Serve with the cottage cheese, breadsticks and crackers.

Leek and Goat Cheese Quiche

Recently, on a transatlantic crossing on the Queen Mary 2, I received an e-mail from a friend who said that on that particular night, he knew the chef would feature a delicious Leek and Goat Cheese Tartlet. He insisted that I try the quiche and then try to figure out how to make it. Here is what I've come up with and it has been very well received as an appetizer or starter.

8 servings

2 medium leeks, washed thoroughly and cut into ½ inch diced pieces (about 2 cups)

2 tablespoons unsalted butter

2 large eggs

2 large egg yolks

¾ cup whole milk

¾ cup heavy cream

½ teaspoon table salt

½ teaspoon ground white pepper

pinch of freshly grated nutmeg

4 ounces mild goat cheese broken into ½ inch pieces

1 (9 inch) partially baked pie shell (warm), baked until light golden brown, 5 to 6 minutes

Adjust oven rack to center position and heat oven to 375°. Sauté white parts of leeks in butter over medium heat until soft, 5-7 minutes. Meanwhile, whisk all remaining ingredients except goat cheese in medium bowl.

Spread goat cheese and leeks evenly over bottom of warm pie shell and set shell on oven rack. Pour in custard mixture to ½ inch below crust rim. Bake until lightly golden brown, and until a knife blade inserted about one inch from the edge comes out clean, and the center feels set but soft like gelatin, 32 to 35 minutes. Transfer quiche to rack to cool. Serve warm or at room temperature.

Polenta Squares with Spicy Bolognese

I took my Grandmother's polenta and, with a little ingenuity, I made it into an hors d' oeuvre for my catering business. I once served it to the Bishop of Scranton. Thanks, Gram!

Makes about 48 - 60 pieces

5½ cups water

1 teaspoon salt

½ teaspoon of white pepper

1¾ cups yellow cornmeal

½ cup grated Parmesan

¼ cup grated Locatelli

½ cup of shredded Fontina cheese

½ stick unsalted butter

4 tablespoons of canola oil for frying

Chopped parsley for garnish . . . .or grated Parmesan cheese for garnish

4 cups Joseph's Easy Spicy Bolognese Sauce (See Recipe Section)

Bring the water to a boil in a large saucepan. Add 1 teaspoon of salt. Gradually "rain" in the cornmeal and whisk with a wire whisk. Reduce the heat to low and cook until the mixture thickens. Stirring with a wooden spoon, you will see the cornmeal getting tender, 12- 15 minutes. Remove from the heat. Add the cheeses, butter, and pepper. Pour the mixture into two 9 x 13 inch baking pans that have been well buttered or oiled.

It is important when pouring the polenta into the pan that you carefully observe that the polenta does not come up more than ½ to ¾ of an inch in the pan. The thicker the polenta height in the pan, the more awkward it will be as an hors d' oeuvre. Thicker pieces are fine for a first course appetizer. Level the polenta in the pans and then chill for about 2 hours in the refrigerator. Take the pans out of the refrigerator and carefully cut the polenta into squares about the size of a 1 inch cube. Heat some canola oil in a sauté pan and sear each square of polenta on one of the 1 inch sides only. Place the seared pieces (seared side up) on a baking sheet and hold until service. Place the baking sheet in a 350° oven for about 15 minutes.

Put about 1 teaspoon of the Joseph's Easy Spicy Bolognese Sauce on each square and put the square in a 1 inch or slightly larger cupcake paper or foil.

Garnish with some chopped parsley and/or grated Parmesan cheese and serve straight away.

SALADS AND SLAWS

Caprese Nicoise

Almost a contradiction in terms! The isle of Capri is known for its dishes with basil, tomato and buffalo mozzarella; however, this is an adaption of a dish I enjoyed in Nice, France.

Serves 2

1 fresh beefsteak or other quality tomato sliced into ¾ inch slices

Fresh buffalo mozzarella, about 3 slices ½ inch thick

4 fresh basil leaves

2 tablespoons of extra virgin olive oil (Combine the basil leaves and oil in mortar and pestle or in a blender to make basil oil.)

Sea salt

Freshly grated black pepper

Stack the cheese and tomato slices alternately. Drizzle with the basil oil, then salt and pepper to taste. Use additional basil leaves to garnish. Serve some crusty French bread to sop up the juices.

Eggplant Caprese

A variation of the Caprese Nicoise and of course, Kaye Ballard's favorite!

Serves 4

1 medium eggplant sliced into ½ inch slices, purged of their water

1 teaspoon of Kosher salt

½ teaspoon black pepper

½ cup flour

4 eggs beaten and thinned with 2 tablespoons water or milk

2 cups Italian seasoned bread crumbs

2 large Beefsteak tomatoes sliced ½ inch thick

4 to 6 slices of buffalo mozzarella

½ cup of canola oil and ½ cup extra virgin olive oil

Basil leaves or chiffonade

Balsamic Glaze (See Recipe Section)

Slice the eggplants into ½ inch slices. Place on cutting board over sink; sprinkle with salt. Place a piece of wax paper or parchment over slices and weigh down with clean bricks or heavy cans. Let eggplants purge for about 25 minutes. The water will run off sides of board. After eggplants are purged, pat dry with paper towels.

Set up breading station with three pie plates. Add flour to one with a bit of salt and pepper. Beat eggs with water in second pie plate. (You can add a handful of parmesan cheese to egg batter if you like.) Place seasoned Italian breadcrumbs in third plate.

Dip eggplant slices first in flour, then in eggs, then in breadcrumbs. Be sure to cover completely, press down on each side of eggplant in crumbs. Place breaded eggplant slices in single layer on large plate or sheet pan. Refrigerate for about 20 minutes so breading will set.

Heat oil in cast iron or other heavy bottomed skillet until oil is shimmering, but not smoking. I always take a pinch of the breadcrumbs and add it to the oil. If the bread crumbs bubble and sizzle, the oil is hot enough. Fry the breaded eggplant slices in batches, single layer until golden on each side. Be sure to adjust heat on stove so as not to burn breading. If oil is not hot enough, breading will not crisp, but will get soggy.

Drain on brown paper bags or wire rack. I don't like paper towel; it creates steam. Let eggplants sit until room temperature or slightly warm. When cooled, arrange one slice of eggplant with one slice tomato and one slice cheese.

Repeat the pattern until all the slices are arranged. Have each slice slightly overlap the next so as to make a circular design on plate or small platter. You can tuck whole basil leaves in between the slices or you can chop the basil into a chiffonade and sprinkle it over the platter just before serving. I like it best when the eggplant is slightly warm and crisp!

Drizzle with Balsamic Glaze and serve. If necessary, you can chill the Caprese and later take it out of the refrigerator and set it out to room temperature.

Greek Salad from Mykonos

Adapted from a salad I had during my visit to Mykonos

Serves 2

1 hot house cucumber chopped into large pieces

1 large vine ripe tomato cut into pieces

¼ of a red onion thinly sliced

½ green bell pepper chopped

½ pound cubed feta

Dressing

Juice of one lemon

4 tablespoons of good quality extra virgin olive oil

2 teaspoons of dried oregano

Salt and pepper to taste

Whisk all ingredients in a small bowl and pour over salad

Joseph's Cole Slaw

The secret ingredient is the sweetened condensed milk. It adds sweetness set against the tartness of the vinegar and makes the slaw creamy as well.

Serves 8

1 large head of cabbage

1 small white onion finely grated

1 cup of shredded carrots

1 cup of good quality mayonnaise

¼ cup of sweetened condensed milk

2 tablespoons of white vinegar

1 tablespoon of celery seed

Salt and freshly ground black pepper to taste

Remove the core from the cabbage. You can shred the cabbage by using the shredder blade of a food processor. I do not recommend using the cutting blade as this will "mince" the cabbage which, in my opinion, is sometimes the texture found in coleslaw, but not my favorite. Peel and shred the carrot on a box grater, or using the shredding blade of the food processor, grate the onion on the small grate of a box grater. You can pulse the onion in a food processor with the steel blade but be careful not to over process and end up with "soup." In a bowl, combine the mayonnaise, sweetened condensed milk, white vinegar and celery seed and pour over the slaw. Season with salt and pepper. Cover and refrigerate for at least 2 hours to chill and let the flavors combine.

My Grandfather's Green Bean and Potato Salad

A cold salad my grandfather made from the bounty of his garden. It is a great summer dish.

Serves 4

2 pounds of Italian flat (Romano) beans, washed and trimmed

4 white potatoes, peeled and cut into large dice

4 cloves of garlic sliced into slivers

10 fresh mint leaves

½ cup good extra virgin olive oil

¼ cup white vinegar

1 teaspoon sugar

1 teaspoon salt

½ teaspoon fresh grated black pepper

Cook beans in a saucepan half filled with water for about 10-15 minutes. Beans should be tender, crisp; drain but do not rinse. Cook diced potatoes in boiling water until knife tender; drain but do not rinse. Combine warm beans and potatoes in bowl. Whisk together oil, vinegar, sugar, salt and pepper. Pour the dressing over beans and potatoes and toss. Add slivers of garlic and break up mint leaves with your fingers and add to salad. Toss, cover and chill for at least 2 hours. Serve cold.

Red Cabbage and Mango Slaw

This tangy slaw also makes a great topping for burgers and even fish tacos!

Serves 8

½ cup rice wine vinegar

1 cup of good quality extra virgin olive oil

2 tablespoons of sugar

1 Bermuda onion julienned

1 large mango julienned

2 tablespoons best quality mayonnaise

1 tablespoon Dijon mustard

Salt and freshly ground pepper to taste

1 medium head red cabbage, finely shredded

2 red peppers finely julienned

Chopped parsley or cilantro

Place vinegar, mayonnaise, sugar and mustard in a blender and blend until smooth. With the motor still running, slowly add the olive oil until emulsified. Season with salt and pepper to taste.

Combine the cabbage, Bermuda onion, mango and red peppers in a large bowl. Add blender mixture. Season with salt, pepper and chopped herbs. Let sit 10 minutes before serving.

SOUPS

French Onion Soup

Inspired by—-but even better than "La Potagerie" in New York

4 to 6 Servings

4 pounds of peeled Spanish or white onions thinly sliced

2 ounces of butter

4 tablespoons of all-purpose flour

2 teaspoons dried thyme leaves

2 tablespoons of canola oil

3 quarts of good beef stock

1 quart of good chicken stock

¾ cup Applejack Brandy

Salt and pepper to taste

8 to 12 pieces of sliced Gruyère cheese or Swiss cheese

4 to 6 pieces of thick sliced toasted French bread

Sauté onion in melted butter and oil in a medium sized heavy bottomed sauce pan. Start on medium heat and stir frequently until onions are soft, then lower the heat and continue to cook for about ten minutes. Do not disturb onions during this time. Then, stir occasionally allowing the onions to caramelize and brown. Adjust heat so as not to burn onions. When onions are sufficiently softened and browned (about 20 minutes) sprinkle the flour over the onions, add the dried thyme, cook for additional 2 minutes, deglaze the pan with Apple Jack Brandy, and then add the stocks. Let the soup simmer and develop (about 30 minutes). Season with salt and pepper. Ladle a generous portion of soup in each ovenproof soup bowl or crock. Top with a piece of toasted French bread and add a generous portion of sliced Gruyère or Swiss cheese. Bake crocks in a 350º oven until cheese melts or place under broiler and melt and brown cheese.

Italian Minestrone

This is a very hearty soup that can almost be a meal when served with my white or French bread and any salad.

10 servings

2 cups of small diced carrots

2 cups of small diced celery

1 cup of small diced zucchini

1 cup of small diced yellow squash

2 cups of small diced onion

2 cloves of minced garlic

2 small potatoes, peeled and diced small

4 tablespoons of extra virgin olive oil

8 cups of chicken stock (preferably homemade)

4 cups of plum tomato (canned, hand crushed with juice)

1 bay leaf

2 small cans of cannellini beans rinsed

1 small can of kidney beans rinsed

1 tablespoon Italian seasoning

½ pound ditalini pasta

Salt and pepper to taste

Sweat carrots, celery, zucchini, yellow squash and onion in olive oil until translucent. Add garlic and sauté 1 minute. Add potatoes and tomatoes, stock and bay leaf. Simmer about 20 minutes. Add beans and Italian seasoning. Simmer 10 minutes. Add dry pasta. Simmer until pasta is cooked, about 6-8 minutes. Garnish with fresh grated Parmesan cheese and a drizzle of extra virgin olive oil.

Mrs. Williams' Meatball Stew

This is a dish prepared by Mary Ann's mother while Mary Ann and I were dating, and one we continued to enjoy after we were married. Not really a soup but more of a stew, it has all the warmth and comfort of a good soup. As Mary Ann's family had emigrated from Avelia, a city in the province of Avellino, in the Campania region of Italy, I tease Mary Ann that this dish is a country specialty. I nicknamed it "vittles." Unlike Mary Ann, I am of Calabrese ancestry, with family in Calabria, a region in the South of Italy located in the "toe" of the Italian boot shaped peninsula. Avelia is further north of Calabria and I am rather opinionated about which region has the better cuisine. Nevertheless, I share this recipe with you. Regardless of its origin, this dish is still very good eats! Notice that I use my grandfather's meatball recipe. Viva Calabria!

8 to 10 Servings

Use My Grandfather's Meatball Recipe (See Recipe Section). However, make each meatball about the size of a golf ball. In this manner, the recipe will yield about 48 meatballs. It is best if you bake the meatballs on a sheet pan for about 20 minutes in a 350º oven rather than fry them as Mrs. Williams used to do.

1 small onion finely diced

4 cloves of minced garlic

4 tablespoons of extra virgin olive oil

4 boiled potatoes, peeled and cut into large pieces

4 pounds of flat green beans or pole beans, trimmed and blanched

4 large cans of San Marzano or good quality plum tomatoes crushed

Salt and pepper to taste

Sauté the onion in the olive oil, then add the garlic and add the crushed tomatoes. Bring sauce to a boil. Reduce heat and add the semi-cooked meatballs and let them simmer for about an hour. Add the blanched green beans and potatoes. Season with salt and pepper and cook for an additional 15 minutes or until the potatoes are tender. Serve or chill and reheat.

It tastes even better the following day.

My Grandfather's Fusilli e Ceci

This hearty pasta fagiole was always served on March 19, the feast of St. Joseph. My grandfather made the pasta and rolled it on small, long wires. I used imported dried fusilli, long curly noodles that I break in half and cook. Then I add the cooked pasta to the soup.

Serves 6 to 8

¼ cup good quality olive oil

1 large onion medium dice

5 garlic cloves minced

3 cups of crushed plum tomatoes

4 cups of dried cooked chickpeas or two 15 ounce cans chickpeas drained and rinsed

4 cups of chicken broth preferable home made

1 pound of dry fusilli broken in half and cooked al dente

Salt and pepper to taste

Pinch of dried oregano

Crushed red pepper to taste

Heat olive oil over medium heat in large sauce pan. Sauté onion until it is translucent. Add garlic and sauté briefly; do not burn. Add tomatoes and bring to boil. Let simmer gently while you cook the pasta in salted boiling water. With a slotted spoon, remove cooked pasta from boiling water and add to the tomato mixture. Add chickpeas and chicken broth, salt, pepper and crushed red pepper and oregano. Reduce heat and let simmer for about 10 minutes. Serve with grated cheese.

My Grandfather's Minestra

This is a dish I never really appreciated until I went to Italy at age 24 and ate it on the Autostrada between Pisa and Florence. The meal brought tears to my eyes as I thought of my grandfather making it for me at home, just the way he had learned in the old country.

Serves 8 to 10

2 large bunches of escarole

2 large bunches of endive

4 carrots peeled and cut into half moons

4 cloves of garlic chopped finely

6 cups of cannellini beans (either dried beans cooked, or canned beans drained and rinsed)

½ cup good quality olive oil

2 cups of good chicken stock or water

Salt and pepper to taste

Grated Pecorino Romano cheese

Wash and chop escarole and endive thoroughly, removing all sand and dirt. Change water and soak cleaned greens several times, and then drain in colander. Heat olive oil over medium heat in large saucepan; add garlic and sauté for 2 minutes. Do not burn. Add cleaned and drained greens and toss in the pan. Turn heat low and allow greens to wilt about 10 minutes. Add chicken stock or water, carrots, salt and pepper. Cover saucepan; gently simmer and let cook for about 30 minutes. Add beans and cook uncovered for another 15 minutes. Serve with plenty of grated Pecorino Romano cheese.

My Mother's Chicken Soup

Known to have medicinal qualities, mainly love and affection!

Serves 10

1 pound chicken parts (wings, necks, and bones)

4 stalks celery, including leafy tops, cut into 3-inch pieces

2 whole chickens- washed and rinsed

2 large whole onions, unpeeled

4 large whole carrots, peeled

10 sprigs of fresh parsley

2 teaspoons salt

¼ teaspoon pepper

1 bunch dill

For later:

5 cups of diced carrots

5 cups of diced celery

1 whole onion diced

1 (28 ounce) can of Italian plum tomatoes, drained and coarsely chopped

¼ cup of fresh parsley chopped

Salt and pepper to taste

Pour 16 cups of cold water into a large stockpot, add the chickens and the chicken parts to the pot. Bring to a boil.

Reduce heat, and simmer gently for one hour. Do not let the soup boil. It must simmer gently with very slight bubbles erupting now and then. After the hour, remove chickens from the pot, and set aside on a large platter. Leave chicken parts in the pot.

When chickens cool, remove skin and bones and cut meat into bite-size pieces. Save meat and return all the other bones to the simmering pot. Add onions, carrots, celery, (not the ones for later!) herbs, salt and pepper. Let the soup simmer for another 3 hours and 15 minutes.

Strain the soup, and discard all solids. Add more salt and pepper, to taste. Now add the diced vegetables and the canned chopped tomatoes to the soup. You may add ½ pound of pasta or rice (1 cup) at this time. My mother used orzo pasta or sometimes rice. Cook an additional 25 minutes until veggies are tender. Sometimes when my father would come home late from work, mom would have the cooked pasta or rice on the side and add it to the soup just before serving. Garnish with parsley and/or chopped dill.

Salmon Corn Chowder

Created for Guest Chef Appearance Holland America Cruise Line ms Oosterdam which sailed to Alaska in August 2011. The dish was so well received that the Executive Chef asked if the soup could be served on the line in the Lido Restaurant. To my delight on the last night of the voyage it was!

If you don't care for salmon, you can add crab, lobster, shrimp or even clams to this dish.

8-10 servings

2 tablespoons of canola oil

½ pound of bacon that has been blanched for 6 minutes and then cooled and cut into small dice

2 large sweet onions cut into medium dice

2 cups of small diced celery

1 cup of small diced carrot

½ teaspoon of dried thyme

½ cup of all purpose flour

3 cups of fresh corn off the cob or you may use frozen

4 Yukon Gold potatoes cut into large dice and par boiled until knife tender

⅔ pound of fresh salmon cut into ¾ inch cubes

1 cup of dry white wine

2 cups of half and half

2 cups of fish stock or vegetable stock

½ cup heavy cream

¼ cup of dry sherry

½ stick of unsalted butter cut into small pieces

2 tablespoons of minced fresh chives

1 tablespoon of fresh chopped dill

Kosher salt and ground black pepper to taste

In a heavy bottomed sauce pan add the oil and sweat the bacon, onions, carrots, celery and the dried thyme. Add the flour and cook out slightly. Add the dry white wine and the half and half and fish stock.

Cook until mixture comes to a boil and begins to thicken. Now add the par cooked diced potatoes. Cook until the potatoes are just a bit more tender. Season with salt and pepper.

Add the salmon and the corn. Salmon will cook very quickly in the hot liquid. Add the heavy cream, sherry and finish with the butter, the chopped dill and chives.

White Pasta Fagiole

I came up with this recipe after becoming a bit tired of Red Pasta Fagiole. I based the technique on a bean soup my mother used to make.

Serves 8 to 10

¼ cup good quality olive oil

1 medium onion dice

4 cloves of minced garlic

1-pound of acini di pepe pasta

4 cups of drained and rinsed canned cannellini beans

1 cup of diced, canned, or torn plum tomatoes, well drained

1 tablespoon Italian seasoning

10 cups of chicken stock

Salt and pepper to taste

4 tablespoons butter softened and then combined with 4 tablespoons of all-purpose flour

Grated Pecorino Romano and additional olive oil for drizzle.

In a heavily bottomed saucepan, sauté onions in olive oil. Add garlic and sauté lightly. Add pasta and toast briefly. Add Italian seasoning and stock. Bring the mixture to a boil and then lower heat and simmer for about 20 minutes. Add beans; return to boil. Add tomatoes. Season with salt and pepper. Return to simmer for about 10 minutes. Add the flour and butter mixture and continue to simmer until the soup has thickened. Serve with grated Pecorino Romano and a drizzle of extra virgin olive oil.

Zuppa Di Vedure a la Roma (Vegetable Soup)

Can you believe I paid $24.00 for a bowl of this soup at the Aldrovandi Palace in Rome? When I returned home, I made a whole pot for about $8.00!

Serves 6-8

¼ cup extra virgin olive oil

1 large onion medium dice

2 stalks celery medium dice

2 carrots medium dice

4 cups of shredded kale or Swiss chard

3 potatoes medium dice

2 medium zucchini medium dice

3 quarts of good quality chicken stock

Salt and pepper to taste

Fresh minced parsley for garnish

Freshly grated Pecorino Romano cheese

Heat the olive oil and cook the carrot, celery and onion, just until they are softened. Add the kale and cook until wilted. Add salt and pepper. Add the zucchini and potatoes, and cook 5 minutes. Add the stock and bring to a boil. Reduce the heat. Cover the pan and simmer for about 25 minutes. Serve soup with chopped parsley and grated cheese.

VEGGIES

Escarole with White Beans

My grandfather called this "scarola." Adding the white beans almost makes it a meal, but it really is a side vegetable dish. You can make the dish without the beans if you prefer. I myself, like to "unto" (translates to "greasy" which means sop the bread in the juices). It's so good!

6-8 servings

½ cup extra virgin olive oil

4 garlic cloves thinly sliced

2 cans of rinsed and drained cannellini beans

3 large bunches of escarole, cleaned and chopped

1 cup water or chicken stock

Salt and pepper to taste

In a deep saucepan heat olive oil and sauté garlic, but do not brown. Add the chopped escarole and either a cup of cold water or a cup of chicken stock. Add salt and pepper. Cover and cook for about 15-20 minutes until the escarole is wilted and tender. Add the white beans and heat through. Adjust seasoning if necessary and serve.

My Grandfather's Giambotta

Giambotta is usually an Italian vegetable stew. This dish is another variation of frittata created by my Grandfather which he named "giambotta!"

8 servings

½ cup finely chopped onion

2 teaspoons finely minced garlic

4 cups of large diced zucchini

½ loaf of day-old Italian bread cubed

1 cup of chopped plum tomatoes drained

2 tablespoons extra virgin olive oil

4 eggs, beaten

2 teaspoons salt

1 teaspoon of freshly ground black pepper

¼ cup of grated Pecorino Romano cheese

¼ cup of grated Parmesan cheese

¼ cup freshly chopped parsley

4 fresh torn basil leaves

In a 12-in. ovenproof skillet over medium heat, sauté onion, garlic and zucchini in oil for 5-6 minutes until zucchini softens. Season with salt and pepper. Add the day old bread, the chopped plum tomatoes, and cheeses. Pour eggs over top. Add the herbs. Continue to cook until eggs are cooked but the mixture is still fairly loose. This dish will not be set as firm as frittata.

My Grandmother's Fried Potatoes

My fondest memory of these potatoes is the time we had unexpected Italian speaking cousins from Canada come to visit. My grandmother quickly fried up 5 pounds to feed everyone!

Serves 6

2 pounds of Yukon Gold, or Red Skinned potatoes, peeled

4 cloves of garlic thinly sliced

Salt and pepper to taste

¼ cup of canola oil and 4 tablespoons of olive oil

Slice potatoes into ¼ inch slices; soak in cold water. Take a large cast iron skillet and heat the oils together until shimmering. Add sliced garlic and lightly brown, and then remove slices from hot oil. Drain potatoes in colander. Pat dry on kitchen towel. Be sure all water is removed. Place potatoes in a single layer into the cast iron skillet and fry undisturbed until a crust begins to form on the bottom. Using a spatula, carefully turn the potatoes so they can brown on the other side. Avoid mixing so as to not break up the potatoes and to ensure a nice brown crust on both sides of the slices. As potatoes brown and cook tender, drain off excess oil and add garlic slices back to skillet. Season to taste with salt and pepper. Serve straight away or keep warm in 200º oven.

My Grandmother's Spinach and Potatoes

What kid eats spinach? What my grandmother made for me as a little boy, I ate all of it!

Serves 6 or one hungry little boy!

2 pounds of fresh spinach, clean and trimmed (*Grandma always used regular spinach, but you can substitute baby spinach.*)

3 Yukon Gold or Red Skinned potatoes, peeled, large diced and boiled until fork tender

6 cloves of finely chopped garlic

¼ cup of good olive oil

Salt and pepper to taste

After trimming and washing spinach, be sure it is dry with very little water clinging to the leaves. In a large Dutch oven or saucepan, heat oil and add garlic, do not brown. Add spinach and sauté for one minute. Add salt and pepper and cook for about 2 minutes. Add cooked potatoes; cover pot and let cook on very low heat for another few minutes until spinach is completely cooked and potatoes are warmed through.

My Mother's Stuffed Artichokes

Most kids hate vegetables!!! I loved these as a child because they were delicious and such fun to eat. You have to take each stuffed leaf and grate it, one at a time against your top teeth to get the "meat" of the artichoke.

8 large artichokes

8 tablespoons extra virgin olive oil

4 cups of seasoned Italian bread crumbs

½ cup parmesan cheese

⅓ cup fresh flat leaf Italian parsley minced

Salt and pepper to taste

1 cup of dry white wine

1 cup of water

2 fresh lemons halved

Cut off the stems and about ½ inch tips of the artichokes. Remove all the tough outer leaves and wash the artichokes. Leave them damp. Using your fingers, spread the leaves carefully open as you tap the artichokes against the counter or table you are working on. Combine the bread crumbs, cheese and parsley in a bowl. Sprinkle the artichokes in and out with some salt and pepper.

Fill the bread crumb mixture between the leaves of each artichoke. Stuff very full. Place the artichokes upright in a large saucepan to fit snugly. If you have a circular rack that fits inside the saucepan, place the artichokes on top of the rack. If you don't have a rack, you will still have good results. Drizzle 1 tablespoon of olive oil over each of the stuffed artichokes and then squeeze the half cut lemons over them being careful to catch the seeds. Add the squeezed lemon halves to the pan. Add the one cup white wine and the one cup water to the sides of the pan to ensure not soaking the stuffed artichokes. Cover tightly with a lid and simmer on low heat until tender, about 1 hour.

Serve with additional lemon wedges if you like.

My Mother's Stuffed Zucchini Boats

At the end of summer when we were just about green from eating so much zucchini from my grandfather's bountiful garden, my mother would come up with new ways of cooking it!

Serves 6 to 8

4 large zucchini, halved with seeds removed

2 pounds of meatball dough (mixture) — (See Recipe Section for My Grandfather's Meatballs)

Good quality olive oil for frying

2 quarts of My Grandfather's Spaghetti Sauce (See Recipe Section)

Grated Parmesan cheese

Salt and pepper to taste

Leave the skin on each of the zucchini. Cut each one lengthwise. Large zucchini from summer's end will have lots of seeds. Make a canal in each zucchini half, using a tablespoon to remove seeds and some flesh. Salt and pepper each half. Stuff each half with about 4 ounces of the meatball dough. If the zucchini is especially long, you can cut each long half into half to make smaller "boats."

Heat about ½ cup of olive oil in skillet. When oil shimmers, place stuffed zucchini meat side down in frying pan. Do not crowd the pan. Let the meat brown for a few minutes and then turn the zucchini on the other side. Allow to brown just for a minute. Remove browned zucchini boats and let drain on brown paper bag or a rack.

Using a Pyrex 13 x 9 or other similar baking dish, cover the bottom of the dish with sauce. Place zucchini boats in baking dish (browned meat side up). Top with more sauce and a sprinkling of grated parmesan cheese. Cover baking dish with foil and bake for 25 minutes in 350º oven. Remove foil and continue to bake for 15-20 minutes until meat is cooked and all zucchini are soft but still holding their shapes.

PASTA

Butternut Squash Ravioli with Brown Sage Butter

This pasta dish says autumn has arrived. It can be served as a first course or as a main meal.

4 Servings

1 small to medium butternut squash (about 2½ pounds)

Olive oil; canola oil for frying sage leaves

2 tablespoons unsalted butter

½ cup mascarpone cheese at room temperature

2 tablespoons freshly grated Parmesan

¼ teaspoon ground cinnamon

¼ teaspoon freshly grated nutmeg

Kosher salt and freshly ground pepper

Flour, for dusting board

4 tablespoons unsalted butter

8 fresh sage leaves; additional 16 sage leaves for garnish

2 ounces Parmesan, for grating

1 pound of fresh pasta dough rolled into 18 inch sheets My Grandmother's Pasta (See Recipe Section)

Preheat oven to 375°. Cut squash in half lengthwise and remove the seeds. Season with salt and pepper and a drizzle of olive oil. Place cut side down on a roasting pan. Cook in the oven until very soft, about one hour. Let cool to room temperature and scoop out flesh with a spoon. Use a food processor, and puree squash until smooth. Spread the puree onto a baking sheet lined with parchment paper and place in the preheated oven for about 7-10 minutes to allow some of the moisture from the squash to evaporate. Remove the puree from the oven and place the mixture in a bowl. Heat the 2 tablespoons butter until it is melted and add to squash with mascarpone, Parmesan, cinnamon, and nutmeg. Season to taste with salt and pepper and mix well. The mixture needs to be covered with plastic wrap and refrigerated for about 2 hours.

I prefer to make the filling the day before I am going to use it, so it is very cold.

To fill the Ravioli:

Lay out a sheet of pasta dough on a lightly floured board. Put 1 tablespoon of squash filling intermittently along the sheet with about a two finger space between each. Leave a ½ inch border all around the filling mounds. Dipping your finger in some water, moisten the top ridge of the pasta dough strip as well as the bottom, and each two finger space between the fillings. Fold the top of the sheet over the filling mounds to meet the bottom and press in between each mound as well as the top and bottom edges. Using a small glass or ravioli cutter, cut each ravioli. Lay all the ravioli out to dry on a lightly floured board or baking sheet and lightly flour the tops. Repeat until you run out of dough and/or filling. Chill the ravioli until you are ready to use. Boil in lightly salted water until the ravioli float to the top. Reserve 2 ounces of the cooking water.

Sage Brown Butter

Fry the 16 sage leaves in about 1 inch of canola oil heated in a sauce pan until 350° for about 15 seconds until brown. Drain on brown paper bags and reserve leaves for garnish. Meanwhile, chop the other eight sage leaves into a chiffonade. While ravioli are cooking, in a large sauté pan, melt the remaining butter with the additional (chopped) sage and add a pinch of salt. Continue to heat until the mixture foams and becomes light brown. On medium heat, toss the cooked ravioli in the sage butter. Transfer to a serving platter or to individual dishes. Add the reserved cooking water to the pan and swirl with any residual butter. Spoon the butter sauce over the ravioli, and then finish with a generous grating of Parmesan.

Gnocchi

Homage to Matilde in Tolfa, Italy, who taught me her method of making potato gnocchi. My grandmother was never fond of making gnocchi, but her sister, my Aunt Aggie, was a master of this pasta. She and Matilde would have been best of friends!

12 medium waxy yellow potatoes

Strong flour (the exact quantity depends on the type of potatoes, the water, the potatoes, and whether the potatoes are new or mature)

Boil, peel and finely rice the potatoes while they are still fairly hot. Allow the potatoes to cool before adding the flour because warm potatoes absorb more flour and make the gnocchi too hard. Add the flour to the potatoes little by little, folding and gently kneading to mix them together to form a very soft mixture. Not too much flour is the trick. You only want enough flour to bind the potatoes into a very soft, puffy ball. It may well feel a little sticky. (You can test whether the gnocchi dough is ready by putting a ball into boiling water. If the ball doesn't break up, the dough is ready.)

Using just a little flour, roll the dough into 12 inch ropes. Then cut the ropes into 1 inch pieces. You can roll these pieces of gnocchi over a grater or a fork to make a prettier shape. Dust in flour and transfer to tray. The gnocchi are ready for cooking. Put a drop of oil into a large pan of boiling salted water. It is important to use ample water to cook pasta. With gnocchi, it is also important to cook them immediately.

Add the gnocchi to the boiling water. Fish them out with a sieve once they come to the surface. Serve straight away with your favorite tomato or pesto sauce and grated Parmesan and pecorino cheese. (For the pesto sauce, see the Recipe Section.)

My Grandmother's Manicotti

My grandmother used to sit at the kitchen table with an electric fry pan to make the tender crepes. In her younger years, she would stand at the stove for hours and use a small cast iron skillet to cook the crepes.

Crepes

3 tablespoons melted butter

3 large eggs

1½ cups of whole milk

1 cup of all-purpose flour

In a bowl whisk together eggs and milk; add butter, and finally flour. When combined——but not overworked——cover and let batter rest in refrigerator for at least one hour. (IMPORTANT: resting for 1 hour makes the crepes tender.) Heat a small crepe pan (8 inch no stick or Teflon works best) or no stick electric skillet to a medium temperature. Brush the pan lightly with canola oil and gently pour about 4 tablespoons of batter into skillet. Form circle or disk shape using the back of a tablespoon or swirl small skillet so that batter evenly coats the bottom of pan. Cook for about 45 seconds or just until crepe is set and then, with a spatula, gently lift and flip to other side and cook for an additional 20 seconds until set. Do not brown. Crepes should be cooked, but pale in color. Remove and place on kitchen sack towel or wax paper. Continue cooking crepes and cooling. This recipe yields about 12 crepes. You can stack the crepes between sheets of wax paper once they are completely cooled.

The Filling

2 cups of whole milk ricotta cheese

1 whole egg

¼ cup of grated Parmesan cheese

½ cup of shredded whole milk mozzarella cheese - plus 4 cups reserved for topping

2 tablespoons of finely minced parsley

Salt and pepper to taste

In large bowl mix all ingredients together (except the 4 cups of reserved shredded mozzarella) until well incorporated.

Making the Manicotti

Lay a crepe on a wooden board or table. Take about 1 tablespoon of the ricotta mixture and spread over half the crepe. Roll the filled part of the crepe over the unfilled half until completely rolled. Place seam side down in a buttered baking 13 x 9 Pyrex or similar type dish. Continue with each of the prepared crepes. Cover with about 4 to 6 cups of My Grandfather's Spaghetti Sauce. (Recipe Section) Sprinkle with generous portion, about 4 cups of shredded mozzarella cheese. Cover baking dish with foil. Bake in 350° oven for about 15 minutes. Uncover dish and bake another 8 minutes until bubbly.

My Grandmother's Pasta

My grandmother made homemade pasta for every holiday and most Sundays! In Italy, the relatives roll the pasta by hand. My grandmother used a hand crank pasta machine that my grandfather brought from the old country.

Serves 4

1 pound all-purpose flour

4 eggs

1 tablespoon olive oil

Place flour into a mound on a large wooden board. Make a well in the center of the flour and then add eggs. (Break each egg separately in small bowl and add to flour one at a time to ensure that you don't have a bad egg.)

Take a fork and beat the eggs in the center of the flour mound and break yolks. Add oil to beaten eggs and beat with fork to combine. Working along the walls of the flour with the fork, begin to combine flour with the wet ingredients. Continue with fork in circular motion as the walls of the flour collapse and enough of the flour is incorporated into the liquid to prevent it from running off the board. Using your hands, begin to work the flour and eggs until a sticky dough forms. Once you have a sticky ball, let it rest while you wash your hands. Taking additional flour, knead the dough with the heels of your hands for about 15 minutes. The dough will begin to get more elastic and take on a bit of a gloss. Take the kneaded dough and wrap in plastic wrap or wax paper and let it rest for another fifteen minutes. Roll and cut in a pasta machine. Heat up a pot of lightly salted water and boil pasta until al dente.

Pacheri Alle Melanzane

My version of a poorly prepared dish I had in Rome after the waiter forgot to bring my dinner! This is truly an example of taking a bad dish and making it good. Enjoy!

4 to 6 servings

1 pound pacheri or penne pasta (cooked al dente)

⅓ cup olive oil, and an additional 2 tablespoons

3 garlic cloves, minced

½ teaspoon red chili flakes (if desired, more to taste)

¼ cup chopped fresh flat-leaf parsley, and an additional ⅓ cup

4 Japanese eggplants, ends trimmed, cut into halves lengthwise, and then cubed

⅓ cup dry white wine

2 tablespoons of tomato paste

2 cups halved cherry tomatoes (red, yellow or a blend)

Extra-virgin olive oil, for drizzling

¾ teaspoon kosher salt

¾ teaspoon freshly ground black pepper

Grated Parmesan cheese

Bring a large pot of salted water to a boil over high heat. Add the pasta and cook until tender but still firm to the bite, stirring occasionally, about 8 to 10 minutes. Drain pasta.

Meanwhile, place a large, heavy skillet over medium-high heat. Add the ⅓ cup olive oil, garlic, red chili flakes, and ¼ cup parsley. Stir and cook until fragrant, about 1 to 2 minutes. Add the eggplant and cook until tender and lightly browned, about 5 minutes. Add the white wine and cook until the wine is almost evaporated, about 2 minutes. Add tomato paste. Turn off the heat. Add the tomatoes, cooked pasta, the remaining ⅓ cup parsley and stir. Drizzle with extra-virgin olive oil and sprinkle with the salt and pepper and a nice dose of grated Parmesan cheese.

POLENTA/RICE

Coconut Rice

This dish goes especially well with Joseph's Asian Grilled Salmon but is also a nice accompaniment with Joseph's Oven Roasted Citrus Orange Glazed Pork Tenderloin. Both recipes can be found in the Recipe Section.

8 servings

1 tablespoon of unsalted butter, plus one additional tablespoon

2 cups of jasmine rice

1 teaspoon of salt

1 teaspoon of sugar

2 tablespoons of finely minced green onion

1 cup of thick coconut milk

1½ cups water

Melt butter in heavy bottomed pan. Add minced green onion and rice. Sweat until onion softens and rice become glossy. Add sugar and salt. Stir. Add the coconut milk and water. Turn heat to low and cover pan. Let rice cook for 20 minutes. Add additional butter and let stand for another 5 minutes covered and off the heat.

My Grandmother's Polenta

My grandmother would make the polenta, pour it steaming from the pot on to a wooden cutting board, and then top it with the sauce and grated cheese. Each person would eat the polenta from a corner of the board. I always liked my own plate!

Serves 4 to 6

6 cups water

2 teaspoons salt

1¾ cups yellow cornmeal

½ cup grated Parmesan

¼ cup grated Locatelli

½ stick unsalted butter

½ teaspoon white pepper

Choose your favorite sauce or one from the Recipe Section such as:

    Joseph's Spicy Bolognese Sauce

    My Grandfather's Spaghetti Sauce

Bring the water to a boil in a large saucepan. Add 2 teaspoons of salt. Gradually "rain" in the cornmeal and whisk with a wire whisk. Reduce the heat to low and cook until the mixture thickens. Stir with a wooden spoon; the cornmeal will get more tender (12- 15 minutes). Remove from the heat. Add the cheeses, butter, and pepper. Serve with plenty of sauce and more grated cheese.

My Grandmother's Thursday Baked Rice

When my wife and I visited relatives in Rome, Italy, my cousin Rosetta used rigatoni instead of rice for the same recipe. Both are incredibly delicious!

Serves 6 to 8

12 cups of cooked rice or 1 pound of rigatoni cooked al dente

2 cups of shredded whole milk mozzarella cheese

6 hard boiled eggs

½ recipe of My Grandfather's Meatball dough (See Recipe Section)

(Roll into 24-36 tiny meatballs and either fry or place on baking sheet to brown; do not cook through.)

3 quarts of My Grandfather's Spaghetti Sauce (See Recipe Section)

3 cups of whole milk ricotta

Butter for greasing pan

Chopped parsley for garnish

Fresh grated Parmesan cheese

Cook rice or rigatoni slightly underdone. Drain but do not rinse. Butter a Pyrex 13 x 9 or other similar stoneware or glass dish. Cover the bottom of the dish with about 2 cups of the sauce. Put half of the rice or rigatoni in the dish. Cover with another 2 cups of the sauce. Place tiny meatballs around the entire dish on top of the rice or pasta. Sprinkle with 1 cup of the grated mozzarella. With a tablespoon, dollop ricotta all around the dish, but do not spread it around the dish. Slice the hard boiled eggs and place them in the dish in a single layer. Top the dish with the other half of the rice. Cover the top layer with 4 more cups of sauce, a handful of grated Parmesan and the rest of the mozzarella. Bake uncovered in 350º oven for 35 minutes. Let dish set for about 15 minutes. Dish out portion and cover with additional hot spaghetti sauce, grated Parmesan and some chopped parsley.

Rice, Dried Cherry, and Almond Dressing

This is a recipe I devised for a Thanksgiving cooking class I taught at Zuppa! It's a great side dish for anytime in the autumn months. I like to add white rice to the wild rice because of the different textures.

About 10 cups

1 cup dried cherries or dried cranberries (about 4 ounces)

⅔ cup tawny or ruby port

1 cup (11 ounces) wild rice, rinsed, plus 1 cup of converted white rice

2 tablespoons butter (additional 3 tablespoons butter if making ahead)

3 medium celery ribs, finely chopped, plus ⅓ cup finely chopped celery leaves

½ cup minced shallots

1 cup (4 ounces) toasted slivered almonds

4 teaspoons chopped fresh sage or 2 teaspoons dried

¾ teaspoon salt

½ teaspoon freshly grated black pepper

¼ cup homemade turkey stock or chicken broth

In a small bowl, mix the dried cherries and port and let stand while preparing the stuffing.

Bring a large pot of lightly salted water to a boil over high heat. Add the wild rice, and reduce the heat to medium. Cook until the wild rice is almost tender about 30 minutes. Add the white rice and continue to cook an additional 30 minutes. Drain well. Place the rice in a large bowl.

In a large skillet, melt the butter over medium heat. Add the chopped celery and cook until crisp-tender, about 5 minutes. Add the shallots and celery leaves and cook until softened, about 2 minutes. Add the cherries and their soaking liquid. Boil until the port has almost completely evaporated, about 3 minutes. Stir the warm rice into the mixture, along with the almonds, sage, salt and pepper. Continue to cook for a few minutes until all the flavors are incorporated and the dish is very hot. Serve.

The dressing can be prepared up to 1 day ahead. To reheat, melt 3 tablespoons unsalted butter over medium heat in a large skillet or Dutch oven. Add the stuffing and cook, stirring often, until warmed. If the dressing is dry you can add about ¼ cup of chicken broth to moisten.

Suppli al Telefono - Arancini - Rice Balls

I had these for the very first time on my honeymoon in Rome. I made them for our family on our return to the States and now these savory fried balls of rice and cheese have become a staple every Christmas. The melted cheese draws out into long "wires" as you break open the rice ball, hence the name, "telephone wires."

6 servings

1 cup Italian-style seasoned bread crumbs set aside for breading

2 cups cooked and cooled Arborio or short-grain rice

½ cup Italian-style seasoned bread crumbs

¼ cup finely grated Parmesan cheese

¼ cup of finely grated Pecorino Romano cheese

2 tablespoons of finely chopped fresh basil leaves

2 tablespoons of finely chopped flat leaf Italian parsley

1 cup of frozen baby peas

1 cup of chopped plum tomato (If you are using canned, drain well; if fresh, remove seeds.)

2 eggs beaten

4 ounces of mozzarella cheese cut into 16 (½ inch) cubes

Canola oil, for frying

Put the 1 cup of bread crumbs in a medium bowl. Set aside.

In a medium bowl, combine the rice, ½ cup bread crumbs, grated cheeses, chopped herbs, and eggs. Lightly mix in the frozen peas and tomato just to combine. With damp hands, using about 2 tablespoons of the rice mixture, form the mixture into 1¾ inch diameter balls. Make a hole in the center of each ball and insert a piece of the cubed mozzarella cheese. Enclose the hole filled with the cheese by rolling the rice ball in your hands into a nicely shaped ball. Then roll the balls in the breading to coat. Refrigerate the rice balls for about 20 minutes before frying.

In a large heavy-bottomed saucepan, pour in enough oil to fill the pan about 6 inches full. (You can also use an electric deep fryer) Heat over medium heat until a deep-frying thermometer inserted in the oil reaches 350° F. Fry the rice balls a few at a time, turning occasionally, until golden, about 4 to 5 minutes. Drain on paper towels or a rack and serve.

SAUCES

Balsamic Glaze

For Kaye Ballard's Favorite Eggplant Caprese!

2 cups Balsamic Vinegar

1 tablespoon sugar

In small saucepan, reduce the vinegar over medium heat. The vinegar should be syrupy.

At the last minute, add the sugar and swirl in hot glaze to dissolve. Cool until warm and drizzle over dish.

NOTE: I like to use the glaze as soon as it cools slightly. If chilled, the syrup will get hard and sticky. It will have to be reheated slowly with a bit of water added. Put the glaze in a squeeze bottle and you can make designs on your guest plates before plating entries- like fish or chicken that would be complemented by this tasty sauce!

Béarnaise Sauce

A classic emulsion sauce that takes a little practice but well worth the time

Makes about one cup of sauce

¼ cup fresh tarragon, chopped

2 shallots, minced

¼ cup champagne vinegar

¼ cup dry white wine

3 egg yolks

1 stick butter, melted

Salt and pepper to taste

In a small saucepan, combine the tarragon, shallots, vinegar and wine over medium-high heat. Bring to a simmer and cook until reduced by half. Remove from heat and set aside. The mixture will be almost dry.

Place a stainless steel bowl in a saucepan containing simmering water, or use a double boiler. Be sure that the simmering water does not touch the bottom of the bowl. Using a wire whisk, whisk the egg yolks until doubled in volume. Whisk vigorously to incorporate as much air as possible into the yolk. The air will act as insulation, so the sauce will not curdle. Slowly add the melted butter in a thin stream, continue beating until sauce is thickened. Stir in reserved shallot reduction. Season with salt and pepper. Keep warm over barely simmering hot water.

Joseph's Easy Spicy Bolognese

This recipe is perfect for the Polenta Squares, but you can use it on any pasta!

Makes about 3 quarts

1 pound of ground beef (80/20)

1 pound of hot Italian sausage meat

¼ cup good quality olive oil

1 cup chopped onion

1 carrot, peeled and grated on coarse side of box grater

2 cloves of garlic minced

1 cup of dry white wine

1 cup of whole milk

4 tablespoons of tomato paste

2 large cans (35 ounce) of good plum tomatoes crushed (Cento or San Marzano)

Salt and pepper to taste

½ teaspoon red pepper flakes

2 tablespoons chopped parsley

2 tablespoons chopped basil chiffonade

In a large sauce pan, heat olive oil over medium heat. Brown beef and sausage together until both are golden. Add onion and carrot; sauté for two minutes. Add garlic; do not burn. Add tomato paste and stir to combine Let cook for one minute until sweet aroma develops. Add one cup of white wine and let boil until almost dry. Add milk and reduce until almost dry again. Add plum tomatoes, salt, pepper, and red pepper flakes. Let sauce simmer partially covered on low heat for about one hour. Add herbs at end. Serve with pasta or polenta. (See Recipe Section)

Matilde's Pesto

Matilde would not agree, but I add a bit of lemon zest and freshly squeezed lemon juice to the pesto and a bit of salt!

6 servings

2 cups of whole basil leaves

½ cup of good quality olive oil

2 tablespoons of pine nuts

2 cloves of garlic, crushed with knife

½ cup of freshly grated Parmesan cheese

Put the basil, garlic, and pine nuts into a food processor. Process and slowly add oil until evenly blended. Mix in the Parmesan cheese.

Optional: Lemon zest and juice about 2 tablespoons, and 1 teaspoon of salt

My Grandfather's Spaghetti Sauce

This was a family staple at every Sunday dinner and holiday! This sauce is an essential part of so many recipes that you should always try to have some in the refrigerator. Preparing it early and often is a great idea.

Makes about 4 quarts

2 pounds of meaty pork bones, or country style spare ribs with bones

1 pound of sweet Italian sausage cut into 3 inch pieces

½ of a whole cut up chicken (optional) *Grandma and Mom liked to put chicken in the sauce.*

12 Grandpa's Meatballs (See Recipe Section)

4-6 braciole (optional) (See Recipe Section)

5 cloves of garlic minced

2 small cans of tomato paste

4 large cans (35 ounce) high quality plum-tomatoes, hand crushed or pressed through a food mill

(Grandpa canned his own tomatoes- so did Mom!)

Enough water to rinse cans

Salt and pepper to taste

1 tablespoon sugar

4 whole basil leaves

½ cup of good quality olive oil

I like to use a 12 quart sauce pan to accommodate all the meat.

In a very large non reactive sauce pan, (heavy bottomed stainless steel is best), heat olive oil and brown meats in stages. First, brown pork bones, then sausages. If you want to include chicken, brown and then add it. Remove browned meats. Add garlic to sauce pan and lightly cook. Add tomato paste and one can of water used to rinse each can. Stir up all browned bits from pan. Cook a few minutes, and then add tomatoes, the sugar and the water used to rinse cans. Bring to a slow boil.

Add all browned meats to the sauce along with salt and pepper. Bring back to a boil, add basil, cover pan and lower heat. Place wooden spoon under the lid of the pan, and partially cover. Simmer for about 2 hours. You may have to add a bit more water if sauce becomes very thick. Add braciole after ½ hour of cooking. (See Recipe Section) Add the fried meatballs after 1½ hours of cooking. Remove bones. Place sausages and other meats on a platter. Sauce is ready for pasta dishes or for manicotti. (See Recipe Section)

Roasted Tomato Sauce

This sauce can also be used on pasta or stuffed pastas. It is also a great sauce for parmesan dishes which call for meats or vegetables. Since it is a bit labor intensive, freeze up several quarts to use when you wish.

12 Roma tomatoes halved and seeded

2 tablespoons of extra virgin olive oil

Salt and pepper

1 onion chopped fine

2 cloves of garlic minced

1 carrot grated or chopped in food processor until very fine

Splash of white wine

4 basil leaves chopped fine

Place halved tomatoes on baking sheet and drizzle with oil and season with salt and pepper. Place in 200º oven for eight hours. Puree the oven roasted tomatoes in the food processor. Sauté onion, carrot and garlic. Add the tomatoes and wine. Cook for about 20 minutes. Add the basil.

Spicy Barbeque Sauce

Another great sauce for pulled pork sandwiches or for grilling chicken

Makes a bit more than a quart of sauce

2 teaspoons of minced garlic

1 small white onion chopped very fine

2 cups of ketchup

½ cup of apple cider vinegar

½ cup of orange juice

½ cup of light brown sugar

¼ cup of honey

1 tablespoon of soy sauce

2 teaspoons of hot sauce

1 teaspoon of ground cumin

Slurry made of 3 tablespoons of corn starch and 2½ tablespoons of water

Combine all ingredients except the slurry in a non reactive saucepan. Bring to a boil and then slowly whisk in the slurry. Simmer just until the mixture comes to a boil, reduce heat and simmer about 20 minutes. If the sauce becomes too thick you can thin it out with a bit more water.

Serve warm with the pulled pork.

Sweet and Sour Sauce

This sauce can be put in a jar or plastic container and kept in the refrigerator for several weeks. It goes great with the pulled pork, but you can also use it to baste chicken when grilling!

Makes about 1 quart of sauce

1 cup of ketchup

½ cup apple cider vinegar

½ cup of water

½ cup of pineapple preserves

½ cup of light brown sugar

1 tablespoon of soy sauce

1 teaspoon of garlic chili paste

1 tablespoon of dry sherry

Slurry made of 3 tablespoons of corn starch and 2½ tablespoons of water

Combine all ingredients except the slurry in a non reactive saucepan. Bring to a boil and then slowly whisk in the slurry. Simmer just until the mixture comes to the boil and thickens.

Serve warm with the pulled pork.

MEATS
BEEF/PORK/VEAL

Beef Braciole

My mother sometimes added the hard boiled eggs to this Sunday sauce staple and sometimes omitted the eggs, just because. My grandmother and grandfather always added the eggs!

4-6 tablespoons of extra virgin olive oil

4 garlic cloves, minced very finely with 1 tablespoon kosher salt

2 teaspoons of freshly ground black pepper

½ cup finely chopped flat-leaf parsley

½ cup grated Pecorino Romano cheese

½ cup grated Parmesan cheese

¼ cup Italian seasoned breadcrumbs

4 hard boiled eggs, peeled and chopped

1½ pounds beef top round, cut across the grain into ¼ inch slices (You can also use flank steak cut into cutlets.) You will get about 4 to 6 brociole.

Pound top round or flank steak to ¼ inch thick between 2 sheets of plastic wrap with a rolling pin, a heavy cast iron skillet or a meat pounder. Combine the egg, cheese, breadcrumbs, garlic, parsley, and pepper in a small bowl. Spoon this mixture evenly over each of the beef cutlets. Starting with a short side, roll up cutlets and tie intermittently with butcher's twine to secure each braciole roll.

Heat a skillet with about 4 to 6 tablespoons of extra virgin olive oil. Brown the braciole on all sides, then add to My Grandfather's Spaghetti Sauce. Cook for 1½ - 2 hours.(See Recipe Section)

When removing the braciole from the sauce, remove string and slice the braciole into ¾ inch disks. Serve with additional sauce.

Filet of Beef Tenderloin

Simply prepared because the beef should speak for itself

Serves 8 to12

1 whole beef tenderloin trimmed, tied (Average weight 5-6 pounds)

2 tablespoons olive oil

2 tablespoons of softened butter

1 tablespoon of Kosher salt

1 tablespoon of freshly grated black pepper

1 tablespoon of steak sauce

1 tablespoon of Worcestershire sauce

1 cup of Madeira wine

Preheat oven to 450°. Dry beef well and rub with olive oil, salt and pepper. Heat a dry cast iron griddle pan or large sauté pan until it is very hot. Sear meat on all sides about 2 minutes per side, top and bottom. If using a smaller pan, cut and trim meat into two smaller and more manageable pieces. When finished searing, place on baking sheet and rub with the softened butter. Deglaze frying pan with Madeira, Worcestershire and steak sauce. Set aside. Roast meat in oven until internal temperature reaches 120° for rare, 130º for medium. When meat is removed from oven, pour wine mixture over the meat and tent for about 20 minutes. Remove string and slice the beef into thick slices.

The Béarnaise Sauce is a lovely accompaniment. (See Recipe Section)

Joseph's Oven Roasted Citrus Orange Glazed Pork Tenderloin

My best friend Tony marinated pork tenderloin in my dressing and roasted it. Of course, I had to jazz it up a bit and devise this recipe.

2 pork tenderloins about 1-1½ pounds each

1 cup of orange marmalade

½ cup of *Joseph's Citrus Orange Vinaigrette* (for basting and dipping sauce) www.soupsforyou.com

1 cup of *Joseph's Citrus Orange Vinaigrette* (additional for marinade)

1 tablespoon of Dijon mustard

2 teaspoons ground fennel

Salt and pepper

Whisk together orange marmalade, ½ cup of Joseph's dressing and Dijon mustard. Set aside 4 tablespoons to baste raw pork. Save additional glaze for dipping or as a sauce.

Season the tenderloins with salt and pepper and the ground fennel, then put the meat in a sealable gallon sized storage bag. Add 1 cup of *Joseph's Citrus Orange Vinaigrette* and seal bag. Marinate in refrigerator for 30 minutes. (See page 37)

Remove pork from marinade and sear in hot sauté pan with a little olive oil until brown on all sides.

Place seared tenderloins on wrack with baking pan or sheet and roast in 400° oven for 12-15 minutes until the meat measures an internal temperature of 145°. During the last 5 minutes, brush with 2 tablespoons of the reserved orange marmalade mixture.

Remove from oven; tent with foil. Let pork rest about 20 minutes. Slice the pork into ½ inch diagonal slices. Heat the remaining orange glaze until warm and serve with pork.

My Grandfather's Meatballs

My absolute favorite! Once you eat these they will be your favorite as well. My grandmother's and my mother's meatballs were also delicious, but my grandfather was the Iron Chef of his time!

24 meatballs

1 pound of ground beef (My grandfather used chuck!)

½ pound ground pork

½ pound ground veal

3 eggs

½ cup grated Parmesan cheese

½ cup grated Pecorino Romano

3 tablespoons of chopped flat leaf Italian parsley

8 large basil leaves chopped

3 cloves of garlic minced

½ loaf of day-old Italian bread soaked in water and then squeezed dry

1 cup water

Salt and pepper to taste

2 cups of canola oil

Combine the pork, the veal and the beef in a large bowl. Add eggs, cheeses, herbs, garlic and moistened bread. Mix with your hands, and then add salt and pepper. Add water slowly just to make the meat mixture moist. (You may not use all the water.) Form meatballs; set them on a plate. In a cast iron skillet, heat oil to approximately 350°. Oil will shimmer but not smoke. Fry meatballs in single layer; you may have to fry the meatballs in batches. Watch carefully so as to gently brown bottom of meatballs but not burn them. Oil may also foam. When bottoms of the meatballs are golden brown, turn them with a fork to cook the other side. When browned, remove and drain on brown paper bag. Fried meatballs taste best right out of the oil and drained. If adding to sauce, fry meatballs to light golden on both sides; they will not be cooked through. Add to simmering sauce and cook for about 30 minutes.

My Grandfather's Veal Cutlets

My grandfather sometimes made these with venison, but always told me it was veal!

Serves 4 to 6

2 pounds of veal cutlets pounded thin. (Each veal scallop should weigh about 4 to 6 ounces)

¾ cup all-purpose flour

4 eggs

2 cups of fresh bread crumbs made from hard Italian bread

1 tablespoon of dried parsley flakes

2 tablespoons of grated Locatelli cheese

Salt and pepper to taste

1 cup of canola oil and ¼ cup good olive oil

Fresh lemon wedges

You can make the bread crumbs using a food processor, but my grandfather used the coarse side of a box grater.

You need three containers (pie plates or shallow bowls) for the breading. Place the veal cutlets between two sheets of wax paper and using a rolling pin, pound to ¼ inch thickness. In the first container, combine the flour, salt and pepper. In the second container, beat eggs, add cheese and a bit more pepper. In the third container, combine bread crumbs with parsley flakes. Dredge veal cutlets in flour, then in egg mixture, then press flat on each side into bread crumbs being sure to coat evenly and completely. Heat oils in cast iron skillet and fry in batches of single layer until golden brown on one side, then flip and brown the other side. Be sure to flip cutlet only once. Drain on brown paper bags. Serve with lemon wedges.

My Mother's Swiss Steak

This is another electric skillet favorite that I fondly remember. This one has a hint of Italian seasoning!

Serves 4

4 cube steaks

¼ cup flour

2 teaspoons salt

1 teaspoon black pepper

2 teaspoons garlic powder

2 teaspoons dried oregano (You might use a bit more depending on your taste for oregano.)

1 large onion, thinly sliced

¼ cup Chianti or other Italian dry red wine

1¼ cups of stewed tomatoes

½ cup of good quality olive oil

In a pie plate, combine flour, salt, pepper, garlic powder and mix with fork. Dredge steaks with the seasoned flour mixture, pressing the flour well into the meat with your hands. In an electric skillet, heat oil to 350°. Brown steaks in a single layer on both sides. Remove steaks from skillet and put on a plate. Drain excess oil from pan and add onions; sauté until translucent. Add wine and deglaze pan being sure to pick up all bits with wooden spoon and continue to reduce for about 2 minutes. Add stewed tomatoes and bring to boil. Reduce heat to about 250-300º and place steaks back into the skillet. Sprinkle steaks with dried oregano. Cover skillet and slowly simmer steak for 2 hours. Check skillet periodically to ensure that heat is adjusted to keep a slow simmer. If necessary, add a bit of water or beef stock if liquid evaporates too quickly. During the last 15 minutes of cooking, prop wooden spoon under lid and continue to cook. Skim fat from surface. Taste sauce and season with additional salt and pepper if necessary. Remove steaks and cover with skimmed sauce. Serve.

Pork Saltimbocca

Traditionally this dish is made with veal. When times were tough my grandfather used pork. I think it is even more delicious!! You can buy a whole boneless pork loin, slice what you need and then freeze the rest of the loin for another time.

6 servings

12 pork scallops

1 teaspoon chopped sage

12 slices thin prosciutto

1½ cups all-purpose flour

Olive oil as needed (about ¼ cup)

Salt and pepper

¾ cup dry white wine

1 cup beef broth

6 tablespoons chilled unsalted butter cut into pieces

Lemon wedges

Chopped parsley

Season meat with salt, pepper, sage, and top with one piece of prosciutto per pork scallop.

Place one pork scallop between sheets of plastic wrap. Using a cleaver or rubber mallet, pound and flatten to thickness of ⅛ inch- repeat with pork slices.

Dredge pork in flour. Shake off excess. Sauté in large skillet over medium heat with enough olive oil to coat the bottom of the pan, 2-3 minutes per side. Transfer pork to platter. Pour off fat from skillet and discard. Add wine to skillet and bring to boil to deglaze pan. Boil until reduced by ½, add the beef broth, simmer 3-4 minutes. Reduce heat to low and whisk in 6 tablespoons of butter 1 tablespoon at a time. Season sauce with salt and pepper and chopped parsley. Serve with lemon wedges.

Pulled Pork

We sell so many of these sandwiches at Zuppa!! Don't forget to try the Sweet and Sour or BBQ sauce to top your sandwiches. (See Recipe Section)

Serves 8-10

1 (5-7) pound Boston pork butt

½ cup brown sugar

1 tablespoon kosher salt

2 teaspoons of fresh ground black pepper

½ cup of apple cider vinegar

1 cup ketchup

½ cup of good quality barbeque sauce

1 teaspoon of cayenne pepper

Score the fat cap of the meat by making diagonal cuts into the fat. Make cuts in opposite directions to create diamond shapes on the fat cap.

Mix the brown sugar, the salt, pepper and cayenne together and then rub all over the meat.

Put the meat into a Dutch oven or electric counter top roaster. Mix the apple cider vinegar, ketchup and barbeque sauce together and put over the meat. Put ½ cup of water in bottom of Dutch oven or roaster.

Set the oven or stove top roaster to 250° and cook the meat for 7- 8 hours.

Shred meat with two forks. Place on your favorite roll. Serve with Sweet and Sour Sauce or Spicy Barbeque Sauce. (See Recipe Section.)

Standing Rib Roast

I like to have my butcher remove the bone from the prime rib in one piece. After seasoning the meat, I tie the bones back onto the roast in order to get the full advantage of the meat roasting "on the bone" without having to deal with the bone at carving time. Also the fresh herb mixture is rubbed on the meat between the bones and the meat and does not burn when roasting.

If you prefer, you can roast the meat right on the bone. If you choose to do so, I suggest substituting dried herbs and using garlic powder so as to avoid burning.

6 to 8 Servings

1 rib roast, about 7 pounds

(Be sure the prime rib is completely dry by patting the meat with paper towels before seasoning.)

Olive Oil

Combine:

1 tablespoon of freshly minced garlic

½ tablespoon of finely chopped fresh rosemary leaves

½ tablespoon of chopped, fresh thyme leaves

1 tablespoon of finely chopped fresh Italian flat leaf parsley

1 tablespoon of Kosher salt

2 teaspoons of freshly ground black pepper

Mix the above ingredients in a small bowl. Rub the mixture over the entire roast and then, using 4 or 5 pieces of butcher's twine, tie the bones back onto the meat. Drizzle a bit of extra virgin olive oil over the top of the tied roast. Place the seasoned roast on a rack in a roasting pan. Roast at 425° for 30 minutes. Reduce the temperature of the oven to 325° and roast for another hour or until an instant read thermometer or probed thermometer reaches 120° for rare, 140° for medium rare, and 150° for more well done. Remove the roast from the oven and tent with foil. Let it rest for about 20 minutes.

There will be a "carry over" cooking time after the roast is removed from the oven so the internal temperature (about 10 additional degrees) will rise as the meat continues to cook. Remove the strings and carve slices into the thickness you desire.

Veal Oscar

The first time I ate this dish I was in Aruba!! It is the very first dish I made for a friend's dinner party that was the starting point of my catering business.

4 Servings

12 asparagus spears, ends trimmed

1 pound king crab legs or one pound of poached crab meat

Small bowl of ice water

White wine

Lemon slices

½ cup flour

1 teaspoon salt

½ teaspoon black pepper

8 small veal cutlets, lightly pounded or 4 larger cutlets

2 tablespoons butter, divided

1 shallot, chopped

1 tablespoon fresh tarragon, chopped

1 tablespoon olive oil

Blanch asparagus tips in simmering water, drain, shock in ice water and set aside. Poach crab legs in water, white wine and lemon slices for 5 minutes, then remove from shells and reserve.

Combine flour, salt and pepper; dredge veal cutlets. In a sauté pan over medium heat, melt 1 tablespoon of butter and fry cutlets for a few minutes on each side until golden brown. Remove the veal to a warm platter. Use the same pan, and melt remaining butter. Stir in shallots and tarragon. Add olive oil, asparagus and crab. Sauté 2 minutes just to heat through.

To serve: Place asparagus and crab on top of each cutlet. Drizzle each with Béarnaise Sauce. (See Recipe Section)

POULTRY

My Mother's Fried Chicken

Even though my mother was 100% Italian American and cooked great Italian dishes, her fried chicken is also one of my fondest childhood memories. My mother cooked this chicken in an electric skillet so I have kept the original method in this recipe.

Serves 4

1 chicken (weighing 2½ to 3 pounds), cut into pieces

Salt and pepper to season the chicken

2 cups of all-purpose flour

1 tablespoon of garlic powder

1 tablespoon of onion powder

2 teaspoons of paprika

1 tablespoon of salt

1 teaspoon of black pepper

4 eggs

⅓ cup water

About 2 cups Crisco or canola oil

In an electric skillet, heat shortening to 350°. Beat eggs with water in a small bowl. In another shallow bowl, season flour with garlic and onion powders, paprika, salt and pepper. Wash and dry the chicken with paper towel or kitchen towel and then season the chicken with about a tablespoon of salt and a teaspoon of black pepper. Dip chicken pieces in egg mixture and then coat well in flour mixture. Carefully add to skillet in single batch. May require several batches if necessary. When lightly brown, turn chicken pieces to brown on other side. Be careful not to burn meat. When both sides are lightly browned, place the lid on top of the electric skillet and lower the temperature to 325° and continue to cook covered. Chicken should cook through (white meat about 10 minutes/dark meat 15 minutes). Pierce meat with fork. If juices are clear, the meat is cooked. If you use an instant read thermometer, the internal temperature should read 165°.

My Mother-in-Law's Sunday Chicken

For about 10 years, I ate this chicken every Sunday whenever I had Sunday dinner at my mother-in-law's home. Mom always saved me the wings!

Serves 4-6 people

8 pieces of chicken- 2 wings, 2 legs, 2 thighs, 2 breasts

4 cups of instant biscuit mix

½ cup of milk

4 eggs beaten

2-3 teaspoons of kosher salt

1-2 teaspoon of freshly grated black pepper

1 teaspoon of paprika

2 teaspoons of garlic powder

½ stick of melted butter, plus 1 tablespoon for baking pan

Combine eggs and milk in a shallow dish. Place biscuit mix, paprika and garlic powder, salt and pepper in another shallow dish. Mix. Season the chicken with additional salt and pepper.

Dip each chicken piece in the egg and milk mixture, then in the seasoned biscuit mix. Place the coated chicken pieces on a baking sheet pan greased with 1 tablespoon of butter. A bit more salt and pepper can be sprinkled on the chicken pieces if you like. Then drizzle the melted butter over all the chicken pieces.

Bake the chicken at 350° until the inside of the chicken pieces registers 165° on an instant read thermometer and the chicken is golden brown. Tastes great cold the next day as well!

Pollo Alla Cacciatore

Cacciatore means in the 'hunter style." My grandfather always added green peppers, onions, and mushrooms to his cacciatore. This is Matilde's version that I learned from her in Tolfa, Italy.

Serves 4

8 chicken drumsticks

5 sprigs of fresh sage

3 sprigs of fresh rosemary

2 garlic cloves

½ cup olive oil

¼ cup white wine vinegar

1 cup red or white wine

With a meat cleaver, chop off the nubby ends of the drumsticks. Add the drumsticks to about ½ cup water in a non-stick pan and cook on medium heat for about five minutes. Meanwhile, in a wooden mortar and pestle, pound the garlic, rosemary, and ¼ cup of olive oil until the mixture is chunky and pulpy. (Wooden mortar and pestles allow you to pound and crush herbs better than marble pestles do. If you do not have a pestle, use a food processor and pulse until the mixture is coarsely chopped.)

Drain the water in the pan with the chicken and add ¼ cup of the olive oil and the fresh sage. Stir the chicken around for the first few minutes so it doesn't stick. (Matilde really shook up the chicken with two wooden spoons, almost like a stir fry). Continue cooking for about five minutes.

Add the rosemary mixture to the pan and let it simmer with the chicken for about five minutes. Add the wine and vinegar (Matilde liked red wine in this recipe, but I prefer white wine because it doesn't color the chicken, and it has a clean, crisp flavor.) Let the wine and rosemary mixture simmer together until liquid is silky and chicken is cooked through.

Serve as a main course after pasta.

SEAFOOD

Joseph's Asian Citrus Grilled Salmon

Created for Guest Chef Appearance Holland America Cruise Line ms Oosterdam which sailed to Alaska in August 2011. In Alaska we used Coho, but any good quality salmon will be delicious!

4 servings

2 pounds of salmon fillets

1 cup of *Joseph's Citrus Orange Vinaigrette Dressing* (www.soupsforyou.com)

2 tablespoons of soy sauce

2 teaspoons of sesame oil

2 teaspoons of honey

2 teaspoons of minced ginger

2 teaspoons of minced garlic

1 navel orange cut in half

Salt and pepper to taste

Canola oil

2 spring onions cut into pieces for garnish

In a shallow dish combine the dressing, soy sauce, ginger, minced garlic, honey and sesame oil. Reserve two tablespoons of mixture for grilling.

Season both sides of fish with salt and pepper and place in a shallow dish and dip in mixture on both sides. Let fish marinade in mixture for 20 minutes in refrigerator.

Pre heat grill or grill pan. Oil grill pan or grates of grill with canola oil.

Place fish at 45 degree angle on grates and let grill for about 4 minutes. Turn fish 45 degrees so as to create hatch marks. Let fish grill an additional 4 minutes. Brush top with reserved marinade mixture.

Flip fish to other side on 45 degree angle and repeat same grilling technique for another total of 8 minutes. Brush top of fish with remaining marinade mixture.

When fish is cooked through and flakey, remove from grill. Squeeze navel orange juice over fish and garnish with cut spring onions. Serve over coconut rice. (See Recipe Section)

Joseph's Pan Seared Citrus Orange Grouper

Although my salad dressing was always popular (appropriately enough as dressing for my specialty salads), it wasn't until very recently that I used that same dressing recipe to create a new product. I think the recipe for this preparation of grouper was the result of my recent excitement over having become the proud owner of over a thousand bottles of my newly bottled dressing called "Joseph's Citrus Orange Vinaigrette" which I had developed years before. I needed to come up with an original recipe for my guest chef appearance. That engagement was slated for Holland America's ms Maasdam's 11 day voyage to the Southern Caribbean in December of 2010. The recipe that follows is my marriage between the fruit of the sea and the fruit of my latest creation Joseph's Citrus Orange Vinaigrette.

4 Servings

2 pounds of grouper fillets (one substitute is sole or any other firm white fish)

1 cup of *Joseph's Citrus Orange Vinaigrette* (www.soupsforyou.com)

Segments from 1 whole navel orange

Strips of orange zest

Juice of two whole navel oranges

2 tablespoons of butter, softened

2 tablespoons of canola oil

1 cup flour

2 teaspoons Kosher salt

1 teaspoon black pepper

1 tablespoon of fresh Italian parsley, chopped

Place fish fillets in a shallow dish and pour the dressing over the fillets. Cover the dish with plastic wrap, and let the fillets marinate in the refrigerator for about 20 minutes. Heat the canola oil in a sauté pan over medium heat. Take the fish fillets out of the marinade and pat dry with paper towel or tea towels. Reserve 4 tablespoons of the marinade for the sauce. Season the fish with the salt and pepper and then dredge in the flour. Shake off the excess. Cook the fish in the canola oil for about 7 minutes on each side or until fish is just fork tender and flaky.

Remove the fillets to a platter and keep warm.

Add the orange juice to the pan and 4 tablespoons of the dressing marinade. Allow the sauce to reduce slightly. (It will come together very fast.) Season with salt and pepper. Add the two tablespoons of butter and swirl until melted and creamy. Do not boil.

Spoon the sauce over the fish and garnish with chopped parsley, orange segments, and orange zest strips. Enjoy.

Live Lobster

A contradiction in terms, since the lobsters are dead as soon as they hit the boiling water!

Serves 4

(4) 1½ to 2 pound lobsters

1½ gallons of cold water

1 lemon sliced

2 bay leaves

1 cup of a quality dry white wine

8 peppercorns

In a non-reactive stockpot, place water, lemon, bay leaves, white wine and peppercorns. When the liquid comes to a boil, plunge the live lobsters in head first.

Time for 15 minutes and remove. Serve with drawn butter.

Drawn Butter

Slowly melt one pound of unsalted butter in a 1 quart saucepan.

When the butter is thoroughly melted, skim the clear or clarified butter from the top allowing the white milk solids to settle to the bottom of the pan.

Keep the clarified butter warm until service.

Scallops Sir Galahad

This was another specialty served at Billy's on occasion. I have no idea where the dish came from or, for that matter, the reason for the name of the dish. I do know that I have made it every Christmas Eve since I started working at Billy's.

Serves 4 to 6

Béchamel Sauce

Makes 2 cups of sauce

4 tablespoons of butter

6 tablespoons of flour

2 cups of whole milk

1 bay leaf

¼ teaspoon of freshly grated nutmeg

Salt and white pepper

Melt the butter in a heavy saucepan over medium heat. Add the flour and cook for one minute, stirring continuously. Slowly pour in the milk a little at a time and whisk with a wire whisk as you pour. Once all the milk is added and whisked, stir with a wooden spoon and add the bay leaf, nutmeg and salt and white pepper to taste. Reduce heat to low and let simmer for about 10 minutes, stirring occasionally. Hold warm until ready to use.

Continue with preparation of the Sea Scallops. See following page.

Sea Scallops

2 pounds of large sea scallops

4 tablespoons of butter with additional 4 cuts (small pieces) for topping later

4 tablespoons of dry vermouth

Salt and pepper to taste

¼ cup of freshly grated Parmesan cheese

1 cup of crushed corn flakes

Make sure scallops are very dry by patting them with a tea towel or paper towel. Season both sides of the scallops with the salt and pepper. In a sauté pan (large enough to hold the scallops in a single layer) heat the butter until it foams and add the scallops. (You may have to sauté in batches so as not to crowd the pan and create steam.) Let scallops cook for 3-5 minutes until brown and then flip them to the other side. Allow second side to cook 3-5 minutes. Scallops should be brown and a bit firm to the touch. DO NOT overcook.

Transfer the cooked scallops to a buttered oven proof baking dish. Deglaze the pan with the vermouth and allow the liquid to reduce slightly. Add the reduction to the Béchamel sauce you have previously made. Stir the Béchamel over medium heat just until it reaches a boil. Spoon the hot sauce over the scallops and sprinkle with the Parmesan cheese first, followed by the crushed corn flakes. Place the dish into a 450º oven just until the cornflakes and cheese brown (about 6 minutes), or place under the broiler and brown the cheese/cornflake mixture until light golden.

Serve immediately.

Shrimp Scampi The Best!

I wrote this recipe from memory based on the countless times I saw it prepared, and sometimes had the good fortune to eat at Billy's Seafood and Steakhouse. I believe the ingredients are the same, and most likely the method I observed as well. Without question, the taste I relished is found in this recipe!

Serves 4 to 6

2 pounds of 16-20 shrimp, peeled, cleaned, deveined, butter flied; you may leave the tails on, but at Billy's the tails were removed

¾ cup of all-purpose flour

2 teaspoons salt

½ teaspoon white pepper

3 tablespoons finely minced garlic

½ cup white wine

½ cup chicken broth

1 stick of unsalted butter, cut into small cubes

Juice of 2 lemons

1 tablespoon chopped flat leaf Italian parsley

9 slices of white bread (crusts removed), toasted

½ cup olive oil

Butterfly shrimp by running knife along back and slitting; do not cut all the way through. Press the shrimp down flat so each one opens like a book. Pat the shrimp very dry. Combine the flour, salt and white pepper on plate or in a bowl. Dredge both sides of the butterfly shrimp in the seasoned flour and shake off the excess.

Heat the oil in a large sauté pan until it shimmers but does not smoke. Add the shrimp, opened side down and flat, in a single layer. You have to sauté in several batches so as not to crowd the pan and create excess steam.

When shrimp are lightly browned on the bottom, turn and brown the other side. If the oil is hot enough, the browning will only take a minute or two. The shrimp will begin to turn pink. DO NOT OVERCOOK. Remove them with a slotted spoon; then drain off most of the oil. Add the garlic and cook for a few seconds, do not brown or burn. Add wine and deglaze pan. Bring to boil, and then add chicken broth and lemon juice. Let boil for a few minutes to reduce.

Reduce heat, return shrimp to pan and begin to add the cubed butter. Swirl the pan until the butter is melted, incorporated, and creamy. The sauce should be very hot, but not boiling. Add lemon juice; swirl to incorporate. Place 6 warm toast points (crusts removed) on plate. With slotted spoon, remove 6 shrimp for each plate

Spoon a generous amount of sauce over each serving. Garnish with a bit of the chopped parsley.

Trout Amandine

Serving the trout whole at tableside and then disassembling it for service will show off your culinary abilities, just as I did at Billy's Seafood and Steakhouse!

Serves 4

4 trout cleaned, fins removed, heads and tails on

½ cup flour, seasoned with 1 teaspoon salt and ½ teaspoon white pepper

8 tablespoons butter

½ cup of sliced almonds

4 tablespoons fresh lemon juice

2 tablespoons fresh parsley

Parsley and fresh lemon slices for garnish

Be sure the trout are rinsed and patted dry. Put the flour with salt and pepper into a pie plate or other flat dish. Dredge the trout. Heat 4 tablespoons of the butter in a frying pan over medium heat. When the butter begins to foam, add the trout to the frying pan. Sauté for 6-7 minutes (depending on size of trout) on each side until skin is golden brown. Remove trout from frying pan and put on platter. Squeeze or spoon lemon juice over fish and sprinkle with the 2 tablespoons of chopped parsley. Drain off butter from frying pan and return to the heat. Add remaining 4 tablespoons of butter to frying pan. When the butter begins to foam, add almonds and brown lightly. When almonds are lightly browned and butter is very hot, pour over trout. Garnish platter with lemon slices dipped in parsley. Serve immediately.

Remove head and tail using spoon and fork. Take tablespoon and run it along the back of the trout to split. Flip trout open using fork and spoon. Using the fork, lift the entire bone from the tail of the fish to the head.

Wahu (Wahoo) and Potato Cakes with Red Cabbage and Mango Slaw

Another dish for the ms Veendam and my Holland American Guest Chef appearance.

If you don't have wahu, you can substitute cod. Make the cakes mini and you have a great appetizer.

Yields: 6 very large cakes or numerous appetizers

4 cups cooked, peeled, grated and cooled baked potato (about 4 medium potatoes)

4 cups flaked cooked wahu (about 2 pounds of uncooked fish will yield 4 cups)

¾ cup all-purpose flour; additional 2 tablespoons

6 cloves roasted garlic, or about 1 tablespoon mashed roasted garlic

5 eggs

⅓ cup heavy cream

1 tablespoon of mayonnaise

1 tablespoon of Dijon mustard

2 teaspoons salt

1 teaspoon freshly ground black pepper

1 tablespoon minced fresh chives

4 teaspoons chopped parsley leaves

1 tablespoon of minced Bermuda onion

2 tablespoons of freshly squeezed lime juice

1 cup of plain bread crumbs

4 cups panko bread crumbs

Canola oil for frying

Red Cabbage and Mango Slaw (See Recipe Section)

In a mixing bowl combine the grated potato and flaked wahu and sprinkle 4 tablespoons of the flour over the top. Toss lightly with a fork to blend. In a separate small bowl, mash the roasted garlic cloves to a smooth paste, then add the cream and stir to blend. Add 2 of the eggs and beat lightly to combine. Add the mayonnaise, the Dijon mustard, the lime juice and the minced onion. Stir to combine. Add to the potato-wahu mixture along with 1 teaspoon of the salt, the black pepper, the plain bread crumbs, chives and parsley, and stir to blend well. Line a baking sheet with a piece of parchment paper and portion the potato-cod mixture into approximately 1 cup increments, forming each portion into a cake. This mixture should yield about 6 very large cakes.

Using a standard breading procedure, set out three bowls or pie plates. Combine the remaining flour and ½ teaspoon of the salt in the first bowl. Toss to blend. In the second bowl, combine the 3 remaining eggs, and the remaining ¼ teaspoon salt. Beat lightly to combine. In the last bowl, place the panko bread crumbs. Working 1 at a time, gently coat the cakes first with the flour, and then dip completely in the egg wash. Next, place in the panko and coat completely with crumbs. Return to the parchment lined baking sheet and repeat with the remaining cakes. Refrigerate for about 20 minutes before proceeding.

When ready to cook the fishcakes, heat ½ inch of canola oil in a large skillet and, when the oil is hot (350º), add the fishcakes, in batches if necessary. Cook until golden brown on both sides and heated through, 2 to 3 minutes per side. Transfer to paper-lined plate to drain briefly. Serve hot, with slaw (See Recipe Section) and a squeeze of fresh lime.

DESSERTS

Apple Torta

Another recipe from Matilde in Tolfa, Italy. Perhaps the easiest and best Apple Cake I have ever had!

2 eggs

½ cup vegetable oil

½ cup sugar, additional three tablespoons

Butter for greasing and additional flour

1 cup flour

1 ounce Sambuca

1 heaping teaspoon baking powder

3 tart Granny Smith apples

Powdered sugar

Preheat a convection oven to 325°. Peel and core the apples and cut them into thin slices. Set the apple slices aside. Combine all other ingredients in a large bowl and stir with a fork until smooth.

Butter and flour a 9-inch spring form baking pan. (Matilde used a slightly larger pan with four apples instead of three. I found the 9-inch pan with 3 apples works just as well. Go with what you have.)

Pour the batter into the pan. Layer the apple slices so they overlap. Make sure to push the apples down into the batter so that the apple slices are firmly nestled. You want to pack them in tightly.

Bake for 60 minutes. Cool to room temperature. Sprinkle powdered sugar on top and serve.

Bananas Foster

This recipe was made famous in Brennan's Restaurant in New Orleans during the 1950s.

6 bananas, sliced lengthwise and cut in half (4 pieces per serving)

2 ounces of butter, cut in pieces

2 ounces of brown sugar

1 ounce Crème de Banana liqueur

2 ounces 151 proof rum for lighting

2 ounces dark rum (Meyer's)

Vanilla ice cream – 6 portions

Mix butter and brown sugar in skillet. Cook over medium heat until sugar melts. Slice bananas in halves lengthwise or in quarters and add to butter mixture. Cook until tender. Add liqueur and stir. Pour both portions of rum over the top and ignite. Spoon gently a few times and serve warm over vanilla ice cream.

Mary Ann's Chocolate Pepper Cookies

On the occasion of our marriage, Mary Ann and I were privileged to see the fruits of my grandmother, my mother and my mother-in-law's labors. They used 100 pounds of flour to bake these cookies along with my grandmother's white cookies (Next recipe). They put raisins in the cookies. My wife Mary Ann has come up with this version that is just delicious!

6 cups sifted flour

2 cups sugar

2 teaspoons allspice

2 teaspoons ground cloves

2 teaspoons cinnamon

1 teaspoon nutmeg

1½ to 2 teaspoons black pepper

1 teaspoon baking powder

1 cup cocoa

12 ounces of semi-sweet chocolate chips

2 cups chopped nuts

1½ cups oil

1½ cups water

Mix dry ingredients, add chips, nuts. Add oil and water. Mix well by hand (until soft but not sticky).

Form into balls (tennis ball size).

Bake on ungreased sheets at 350° for 10-12 minutes. Ice with the icing that follows.

Icing:

1 pound of powdered sugar

2 tablespoons of lemon juice

1 teaspoon almond extract

1 teaspoon vanilla extract

Just enough water -- a few tablespoons to make a very thick icing

My Grandmother's White Cookies from Calabria

These cookies are the real deal —-authentically Calabrese, and a staple for every holiday celebration!

4 cups of flour

4 teaspoons baking powder

1 cup sugar

1 cup vegetable shortening

¼ cup whole milk

2 teaspoon vanilla

3 egg yolks

Sift together all the dry ingredients. Using your hands, cut the vegetable shortening into the sifted dry ingredients. Now mix together the wet ingredients and then add them to the dry mixture that has been cut with the shortening. Knead till combined in the bowl.

Use an ice cream scoop or roll into balls.

Bake 375° 10-12 minutes

Ice with same icing used for Mary Ann's Chocolate Pepper Cookies. (See previous recipe.)

Pistachio Cake

I don't know how original this recipe came to be, but my mother always made it, and when I found it among her countless recipes, I started to make it to sell at Zuppa! My mother called a shot glass a jigger.

1 (18¼) ounce yellow cake mix

4 eggs

1 cup club soda

1 jigger of green crème de menthe liqueur

2 boxes (3.4 ounce) instant pistachio pudding, divided

¼ cup vegetable oil

1 pound chopped walnuts

1½ cups milk

1 envelope (1½ ounce) of powdered whipping cream

In a bowl, mix the cake mix, eggs, club soda, 1 box of the pudding, oil, and ½ cup of the nuts. Mix well and bake in a greased and floured bundt or tube cake pan for 45 minutes at 325°. The cake is done when a long inserted toothpick comes out clean. Cool in pan on a rack for 10 minutes. Remove the cake from the pan and continue to cool the cake on rack. When completely cool, place cake on serving plate and cover with the icing listed below. Keep cake in the refrigerator.

Icing:

In a medium sized bowl, mix 1½ cups milk with the powdered whipping cream, and 1 box instant pistachio pudding, along with a splash of green Crème de Menthe liqueur. Using a hand held electric beater, mix on low speed to combine and then on high speed for 4 minutes. Spread on cooled cake and sprinkle with the chopped nuts.

Yum Yum Cake

Another one of those cakes Mom made all the time. I have no idea where this recipe came from, but my mother was well known for making this cake!

12- 16 servings

1½ cups cold milk

1 package (3.4 ounces) instant vanilla pudding mix

1 (18¼ ounces) yellow cake mix

1½ cups whipped topping (Mom always used Cool Whip)

1 can (8 ounce) crushed pineapple, well drained

¼ cup flaked coconut, toasted

In a small bowl, whisk milk and pudding mix for 2 minutes. Let stand for 2 minutes or until soft-set; cover and refrigerate.

Grease the bottom of two 8 inch square baking dishes. Prepare cake batter according to package directions; pour into prepared dishes. Bake at 350° for 20-25 minutes or until a toothpick inserted near the center comes out clean. Cool for 5 minutes before removing from pans to wire racks to cool completely.

Fold whipped topping into pudding until blended. Level cake tops if necessary. Place one cake on a serving plate; spread with half of the pudding mixture. Top with pineapple, and the remaining cake and pudding mixture. Sprinkle with coconut. Store in the refrigerator until ready to serve.

A KISS FROM ABOVE

I should have known, that is, I should have believed that *my sweet, loving grandmother would have had the final word.*

I wanted to include my grandmother's recipe for date and nut bars because I had such a vivid memory of these cookies when I was a youngster. When I was in third grade, I remember a night I forgot to do my homework. I was so distraught that my mother called the Sisters at the convent to explain my distress. The good Sister told my mother to assure me that I could do my homework during recess the following day. I was so relieved! After the phone call, my mother made my grandmother's date and nut bars. Mom told me to take the bars to the nuns at school the next day, but she let me eat one or two before we packed up all the other bars for the Sisters.

As much as I remember that day, I could not remember any such recipe. I was too young. And now, as an adult, for the life of me, I could not find that recipe anywhere, and had no way to reference it. Just a short time before the deadline for final copy of this book arrived, something wonderful happened. I personally know that this event was no accident. I happened to open a notebook in which my wife Mary Ann had copied recipes from my mother and her mother.

A tattered, yellowed slip of paper fell out of the book. There, in my grandmother's own handwriting was the recipe for her Date and Nut Bars

Yet another kiss from above! Grandma was putting her blessing on the book which she had been so instrumental in bringing to fruition from beginning to end. You absolutely must try them. So gently turn the page; she's waiting for you.

My Date and Nut Bars, One of Joseph's Favorites

Makes a bit more than 2 dozen

5 eggs separated

1 cup of granulated sugar

1 teaspoon of baking powder

½ teaspoon of salt

1 teaspoon of vanilla

1 cup of flour

1½ cups of chopped walnuts

1 cup of maraschino cherries, well drained and chopped

1 (8 ounce) package of chopped dates

Powdered sugar

In a small mixing bowl beat the egg whites until soft peaks form and set aside.

In another mixing bowl combine the flour, salt and baking powder.

In another mixing bowl, beat the egg yolks and the sugar until lemony. Add the vanilla. Add the dry ingredients from the second mixing bowl in thirds. Do not over mix. When incorporated add the cherries, nuts and dates. Mix until blended. Then fold in the beaten egg whites.

Pour the batter into a well-greased and floured 10 x 15 jellyroll pan. Be sure the batter is evenly distributed throughout the pan. Tap the pan a few times on the counter. Then bake in a 350° oven for 25 minutes.

When the pan comes out of the oven, sprinkle powdered sugar over the bars.

When completely cooled, cut into bars and dust with additional powdered sugar.

CPSIA information can be obtained at www.ICGtesting.com
Printed in the USA
BVOW060815270912

301511BV00004B/2/P